# WILLIAMSBURG RESEARCH STUDIES

## WILLIAMSBURG RESEARCH STUDIES

# THE ECONOMIC ROLE
# OF WILLIAMSBURG

# The Economic Role
# of Williamsburg

*By*

JAMES H. SOLTOW

COLONIAL WILLIAMSBURG

*Williamsburg, Virginia*

*Distributed by*

THE UNIVERSITY PRESS OF VIRGINIA

*Charlottesville*

19833

FOREWORD

WILLIAMSBURG RESEARCH STUDIES is a series of
specialized reports prepared in the research program of
Colonial Williamsburg.  For almost forty years this program has sought to fulfill a dual objective:  to supply
the day-to-day information essential to the accurate pre-
servation and restoration of Virginia's colonial capital,
and to supplement the interpretation of Williamsburg with
studies broader in scope but as detailed in content.  The
series will make available in inexpensive form those studies
of widest interest to students of the era and locality.

   To inaugurate the series, we have chosen seven
reports from the files of the Research Department.  These
studies originally were for internal use only; some are
largely compilations of the documentary sources relating
to a subject, and others are more interpretive.  Future
titles will appear as research projects are concluded and
will include contributions from the fields of architecture,
archaeology, hand crafts, and the decorative arts.

   For permission to publish certain copyrighted
material in this volume, we should like to express appreciation to Professor Leslie V. Brock, Caldwell, Idaho; the
Carnegie Institution of Washington, D. C.; the College of
William and Mary Library, Williamsburg, Virginia; Columbia

University Press, New York; Professor Calvin B. Coulter,
Tacoma, Washington; The Dietz Press, Richmond, Virginia;
Duke University Library, Durham, North Carolina; the Hall
of Records, Annapolis, Maryland; the Historical Society of
Pennsylvania, Philadelphia; the Houghton Library, Harvard
University; the editor of the Journal of Accountancy, New
York; the MacMillan Company, New York; Mrs. Frances N.
Mason, Gloucester Point, Virginia; the New York Public
Library; the Scottish Record Office, Edinburgh; the Southern
Historical Collection, University of North Carolina Library,
Chapel Hill; the University of Virginia Library, Charlottes-
ville; the Virginia Historical Society and the Virginia
State Library, Richmond; and Mrs. Robert H. Webb, Charlottes-
ville, Virginia.

Edward M. Riley
Director of Research

PREFACE

The importance of Public Times in Williamsburg
is not unknown to those familiar with the life of this
eighteenth-century community.  People from all parts of
Virginia came to the capital four times each year to transact their business as well as to carry on the machinery of
government and to participate in the gala social affairs
which took place at these times.  The purpose of this report is to describe and analyze the role which Williamsburg,
through the periodic Meetings of Merchants, played in the
economy of Virginia.  In other words, the basic questions
are:  What did businessmen do when they came to Williamsburg, and what significance did their periodic assembling
in the capital have in relation to the economic life of the
province?

Any study of the economic history of eighteenth-
century Virginia touches inevitably upon the relations between merchant and planter and upon the conflict between
the business and agrarian ways of life.  If any partiality
is shown here towards the business point of view, it re-
sults in part from the fact that merchants' records were
the major sources for the study.  However, the emphasis
herein is upon the Williamsburg Meeting of Merchants as an

institution which developed to meet the needs of business in a decentralized agricultural economy. As long as Virginians produced goods for exchange (as opposed to production for the exclusive use of the producer), some kind of a system of business was necessary to provide the mechanism for exchange.

A word might be said here about the facilities provided to make this study. The original sources which I used are located in widely-scattered depositories from Edinburgh to San Marino, California. However, all of these manuscripts have been made available in Williamsburg as a result of the microfilming program of Colonial Williamsburg's Research Department. Unquestionably, this has resulted in a great gain in efficient use of time as well as in convenience.

Finally, I wish to express my appreciation for the encouragement extended by Dr. Edward M. Riley, Director of Research, Dr. Richard P. McCormick, special consultant to Colonial Williamsburg, and my colleagues in the Research Department. Thanks also to those who have made available materials at various stages of my research.

James H. Soltow

Williamsburg, Virginia
August 24, 1956.

## A POSTSCRIPT

I prepared the original version of this report when I was a member of the Research Department of Colonial Williamsburg, Inc., 1955-1956. Some of the materials in the report were employed subsequently in writing two articles, "The Role of Williamsburg in the Virginia Economy, 1750-1775," William and Mary Quarterly, October, 1958, and "Scottish Traders in Virginia, 1750-1775," Economic History Review, August, 1959.

Since the preparation of the report and the articles mentioned above, new work has appeared on various aspects of the economic life of eighteenth-century Virginia. I have taken advantage of this scholarship to make revisions of the original study. However, my major conclusion - that Williamsburg and its periodic Meeting of Merchants played a significant role in the decentralized economy of the colony - remains basically unchanged.

J. H. S.

East Lansing, Michigan
March 9, 1964.

TABLE OF CONTENTS

## LIST OF TABLES

# THE ECONOMIC ROLE
# OF WILLIAMSBURG

## THE WILLIAMSBURG MEETINGS

The important way in which events at Williamsburg influenced the political life of Virginia has been widely recognized. After the removal of the capital in 1699 from Jamestown to its new location, Williamsburg was the residence of the governor or lieutenant governor, upholder of royal authority in Virginia; the meeting place of the House of Burgesses, representatives of the colony's property owners; and the seat of the General Court, the highest unit in the province's judicial system.[1]

Neither contemporary observers nor writers of this century, however, have been able to reach agreement on the significance of the community to the colony's economy. A French traveller in 1765 implied that the town was second

---

1. See Carl Bridenbaugh, Seat of Empire: The Political Role of Eighteenth-Century Williamsburg (Williamsburg: Colonial Williamsburg, 1950), p. 78.

in importance in Virginia trade only to Norfolk,[2] while St. George Tucker asserted in 1795 that "there never was much trade in Williamsburg."[3] Lyon G. Tyler wrote in 1907 that "the city was the center of the business interests of the colony,"[4] but Robert W. Coakley concluded in 1949 that Williamsburg's "importance was political not economic."[5]

The economic role of Williamsburg was indeed different from that of the large urban centers, such as Philadelphia, New York, Boston, and Charleston. Each of these centers was the nucleus of a metropolitan economy, in which the wants and needs of the population of the area were "supplied by a system of exchange concentrated in a large city" which was "the focus of local trade and the center through which normal economic relations with the outside" were maintained.[6] These cities were ports for the ocean-going ships

---

2. "A French Traveller in the Colonies, 1765," American Historical Review, XXVI (1921), 741-743.

3. [St. George Tucker], "A Letter to the Rev. Jerediah Morse," William and Mary Quarterly, 1st series, II (1894), 196.

4. [Lyon G. Tyler], "Williamsburg - The Old Colonial Capital," William and Mary Quarterly, 1st series, XVI (1907), 20.

5. Robert W. Coakley, "Virginia Commerce during the American Revolution" (Unpublished Ph. D. dissertation, University of Virginia, 1949), pp. 38, 70-72.

6. N.S.B. Gras, An Introduction to Economic History (New York: Harper and Brothers, 1922), p. 186.

engaged in foreign trade, and through them were funneled
the imports and exports of a hinterland trading area. In
each city, members of the business community performed the
functions of collecting commodities for export and distributing imported goods.[7]

Geography, however, imposed a pattern of commercial
dispersion upon Virginia. The presence of the four great
tributaries of the Chesapeake, accessible for long distances
to most ocean-going vessels, rendered unnecessary the development of a single entrepôt to handle the imports and exports
of the colony. The James River was navigable by the largest
ships of the eighteenth century for a distance of one hundred miles, the York-Mattaponi-Pamunkey for sixty, the Rappahannock for seventy, and the Potomac for 110. Smaller vessels usually could proceed some miles farther to the falls
of each river. In addition, numerous tributaries, particularly

---

7. See Curtis P. Nettels, "The Economic Relations of
Boston, Philadelphia, and New York, 1680-1715," Journal of
Economic and Business History, III (1931), 185-215. W. T.
Baxter, The House of Hancock: Business in Boston, 1724-1775
(Cambridge, Mass.: Harvard University Press, 1945); Virginia D.
Harrington, The New York Merchant on the Eve of the Revo-
lution (New York: Columbia University Press, 1935); Harry
D. Berg, "Merchants and Mercantile Life in Colonial Phila-
delphia 1748-1763," (Unpublished Ph.D. dissertation, Uni-
versity of Iowa, 1941); Leila Sellers, Charleston Business
on the Eve of the American Revolution (Chapel Hill: University of North Carolina Press, 1934).

of the James and Potomac, provided navigation for local craft.[8]

Jefferson's assertion in 1782 that Virginia had "no ports but our rivers and creeks"[9] was more applicable to the seventeenth century than to his own day. The determined efforts of the Virginia government from an early date to foster urban development were thwarted by the Tidewater planters' practice of shipping tobacco and receiving goods at their own landings, which continued through the seventeenth and into the first quarter of the eighteenth century.[10]

By the mid-eighteenth century, small urban centers in all parts of the colony performed much of the business of their immediate localities. Some of these towns, like Cabin Point on the James, Urbanna on the Rappahannock, and Dumfries on an affluent of the Potomac, grew up around the

---

8. Arthur P. Middleton, Tobacco Coast: A Maritime History of Chesapeake Bay (Newport News: The Mariners' Museum, 1953), pp. 31-34; Coakley, "Virginia Revolutionary Commerce," pp. 23-24.

9. Thomas Jefferson, "Notes on Virginia," in The Life and Selected Writings of Thomas Jefferson, ed. A. Koch and W. Peden (New York: Modern Library, 1944), p. 191.

10. Philip A. Bruce, Economic History of Virginia in the Seventeenth Century (New York: Macmillan, 1895), II, 522-565.

tobacco warehouses established by the Inspection Act of
1730.  Others, such as Richmond, Falmouth, Fredericksburg,
and Alexandria, developed as transshipment points at the
fall line of the major river systems.[11]  Only Norfolk, located in a strategic position at the entrance to the Chesapeake, possessed more than local trade interests as a result
of its promotion of the export of grain and other produce
to the West Indies and to southern Europe.[12]  Even so, all
parts of the Old Dominion maintained direct economic communications with Great Britain.

There were other factors, besides decentralization,
which tended to obscure the economic importance of the colonial capital.  Paramount, of course, was the fact that
Williamsburg did not have port facilities, except those for
local craft at College and Capitol Landings.[13]  Had the
capital been located at Norfolk, political and economic
forces would no doubt have combined to give that city an
overwhelming importance in Virginia's life.  Instead, the

---

11.  Middleton, Tobacco Coast, pp. 40-41.  Coakley,
"Virginia Revolutionary Commerce," pp. 24-25.

12.  Thomas J. Wertenbaker, Norfolk: Historic Southern
Port (Durham: Duke University Press, 1931), pp. 28-51.

13.  Tyler, "Williamsburg -- The Old Colonial Capital,"
p. 11.

capital was at Williamsburg, a town whose resident business-men were concerned largely with the retail and service trades. What economic importance it had depended greatly on its political significance.

Four times each year people from all parts of the colony met at Williamsburg - at the sessions of the General Court in April and October and of the Oyer and Terminer Court in June and December. These were the Public Times, when "persons engaged in Business of any kind" were present in the provincial capital.[14] Very obviously, those who had legal matters pending in the colony's judicial system made a regular practice of attending the meetings of the General Court, which held original jurisdiction over all cases involving more than £16 sterling and heard appeals from the county courts in cases of above £10.[15] Furthermore, the Hustings Court in Williamsburg had concurrent jurisdiction over all debt cases in Virginia.[16]

---

14. Governor Fauquier to the Lords of Trade, November 3, 1765. C.O. 5/1331, pp. 54-59, Public Record Office. (Photostat in Research Department, Colonial Williamsburg).

15. Percy S. Flippin, The Royal Government in Virginia, 1624-1775 (New York: Columbia University Press, 1919), pp. 308-309.

16. Calvin B. Coulter, "The Virginia Merchant" (Unpublished Ph.D. dissertation, Princeton University, 1944),

There were many diversions at the capital - horse races, cock fights, the theater - for the merchant or planter who spent much of his time in relative isolation.[17] Luxury goods and services which were not provided elsewhere in the province were available there. In 1775 Williamsburg had six milliners, six tailors, three shoemakers, eight coachmakers and wheelwrights, two saddlers, seven silversmiths and jewelers, seven cabinetmakers, six wigmakers, and three printers.[18] In Public Times, the little capital came to life: "In the Day time people hurying back and forwards from the Capitol to the taverns," wrote a visiting Frenchman, "and at night, Carousing and Drinking."[19]

The court sessions of the Public Times furnished

---

pp. 237-238. Robert P. Thomson, "The Merchant in Virginia, 1700-1775" (Unpublished Ph.D. dissertation, University of Wisconsin, 1955), pp. 279-280.

17. Rutherfoord Goodwin, A Brief and True Report Concerning Williamsburg in Virginia (Williamsburg: Colonial Williamsburg, 1940), p. 36.

18. James H. Soltow, "The Occupational Structure of Williamsburg in 1775" (typed manuscript report, Colonial Williamsburg, 1956). This is a summary of the available data on owners and users of buildings and houses in eighteenth-century Williamsburg, compiled from reports by members of the Research Department, Colonial Williamsburg.

19. "A French Traveller in the Colonies, 1765," pp. 742-743.

the occasions for periodic meetings of merchants and planters from all parts of the colony. Then it was customary for traders to make arrangements for "the Payment of money, Negotiation of exchange &c."[20] Since there was no official gathering place, merchants conducted their affairs in the boardinghouses, in the taverns, and on the streets. One observer reported, not without exaggeration, that in the Raleigh Tavern "more business has been transacted than on the Exchange of London or Amsterdam."[21] Back of the Capitol was an extension of Duke of Gloucester Street, known as the "Exchange," where financial transactions were made.[22]

For residence during Public Times, the tavern near the Capitol, operated by Mrs. Jane Vobe and later by Christiana Campbell, was a favorite because of its location; also, it had a reputation as the place "where all the best people resorted."[23] There were other desirable lodgings,

---

20. John Banister to Elisha Tupper, July 11, 1775, Virginia Magazine of History and Biography, XXVIII (1920), 266-273.

21. "Journal of Alexander Macaulay," [February 25, 1783], William and Mary Quarterly, 1st ser., XI (1903), 186-187.

22. Governor Fauquier to the Lords of Trade, November 3, 1765.

23. "A French Traveller in the Colonies, 1765," p. 741.

though, in the area near the Capitol and the "Exchange."
Mrs. Mary Davis, for example, leased a large brick house
a block west of the Capitol and advertised "12 or 14 very
good lodging rooms with fire places in most of them, which
will hold two or three beds in each."[24] Factors of one of
the largest Scottish tobacco firms engaged lodgings here
in 1770 and considered renting a two-room house behind this
tavern as a place to live and conduct their business during
Public Times.[25]

People travelled to Williamsburg by water and by
land. Those from Norfolk had the choice of two weekly
packets to Burwell's Ferry near Williamsburg. One boat
left Norfolk on Wednesdays and returned on Saturdays, the
other sailed on Thursdays and Sundays. Passage cost five
shillings, for which "the best accommodations for passengers"
were promised.[26] Those from the south side of the James

---

24. Virginia Gazette (Purdie & Dixon), March 22, 1770.
See Mary Stephenson, "Brick House Tavern" (typed manuscript
report, Colonial Williamsburg, 1956).

25. James Robinson to William Henderson, April 17, 1770,
Letterbook of William Cuninghame & Company (National Library
of Scotland), I.

26. Virginia Gazette (Rind), September 8, 1768; September 7 and 20, 1769. The first packet evidently commenced
operations in 1762, the other in 1768.

rode to Hog Island, where they could stable their horses, and used the ferry across the river.[27]

Formal organization of the periodic Meetings of Merchants did not come before 1769. But the rules drawn up in June of that year likely reflect established customs and procedures of business. In the Raleigh Tavern, "a meeting of all persons concerned in the exchange and commerce of this county" agreed "to expedite the mode and shorten the expense of doing business" by adoption of the following set of rules:

> First. That the 25th days of October and April, and the 1st days of the Oyer courts, shall be the fixed days of meeting in Williamsburg for all persons concerned in the exchange and commerce of this county.
> Second. That the time limited for settling the price and course of exchange, and the payment of all money contracts in the General Courts, shall be three days; to begin from the said 25th days of October and April, exclusive of Sundays, and in the Oyer courts from the first days of the said courts to the first Friday in the said courts.
> Third. That all persons who shall engage for the payment of money, or other contracts, in Williamsburg, in the General and Oyer courts, shall be deemed violators of their engagements,

---

27. Virginia Gazette (Purdie & Dixon), October 8, 1772. The advertisement of sale or lease of the property on Hog Island stated that "the Stable only brings, in publick Times, from three to five Pounds a Day, and upwards."

and declared absentees, if not present on the
above first days.[28]

At the Meeting of June, 1770, a Committee of
Trade, with 125 members, was organized under the chairman-
ship of Andrew Sprowle, wealthy Norfolk merchant, "to take
under the consideration the general state of the trade in
this colony." The message "To the Merchants and Traders
in Virginia," issued by the first session of the committee,
outlined the over-all purpose of the organization:

> It has long been a matter of surprise, and
> concern, to many hearty friends to the trading in-
> terest of this colony, that a body of men, respect-
> able as well from their number as the nature and
> extent of their connexions, should never yet (in
> imitation of Great Britain, and other trading
> countries) have formed themselves into a society,
> upon regular and liberal principles; by which
> means they would have had frequent opportunities
> of establishing a confidence with each other, ex-
> ceeding to their interest as individuals, and of
> gaining that dignity in the community to which
> they are so justly entitled.[29]

The Committee, organized in part to formulate the merchants'
policy in the growing controversy between the American colonies and the British government, was similar to the associ-
ations formed at about the same time in the other colonies.

---

28.  Ibid., June 29, 1769.

29.  Virginia Historical Register, III (1850), 79-80,
from Virginia Gazette (Purdie & Dixon), June 28, 1770 (no
known issue in existence.)

New York merchants founded a Chamber of Commerce in 1768, followed by those of Charleston, South Carolina, in 1773.[30]

In the spring of 1771, 168 "principal Merchants" of Virginia subscribed "to an Agreement to meet punctually, for the future," during the General Court sessions in April and October, "and that they expect all those who have any Business with them will meet regularly on these Days."[31]

Again, in November, 1772, it was "unanimously agreed" by the merchants, assembled in Williamsburg, "to engage to meet, and give our attendance in this city, either in person or by our representatives, in the 25th days of January, April, July, and October." A committee, composed of "a select Number of" the body of merchants and chair-maned again by Sprowle, received power to discipline traders who did not attend the Meetings regularly. If the committee judged the reasons for non-attendance to be unsatisfactory, it was empowered to levy a fine of £5 "which is to be applied to charitable purposes." Names of those who refused

---

30. Harrington, <u>New York Merchant</u>, pp. 74-75. Sellers, <u>Charleston Business</u>, p. 73. "The purpose of the New York Chamber of Commerce according to its own prospectus was to promote and encourage commerce, support industry, adjust disputes relative to trade and navigation, and procure such laws and regulations as might be found necessary for the benefit of trade in general."

31. <u>Virginia Gazette</u> (Purdie & Dixon), May 16, 1771.

to pay fines were to be published, "as Persons who do not

pay a proper Regard to their solemn Promises and Agreements."

Merchants from all parts of the colony were represented on

the committee of twenty-eight members, any twelve of whom

constituted a quorum to take action.[32]

No specific account can be given of the origins

of the Meeting of Merchants as an institution.  Ordinarily,

traders visited county courts throughout the colony to pur-

chase tobacco and to settle legal matters.[33]  However,

Williamsburg's political and judicial significance was

colony-wide, and it is not surprising that business dealings

of more than local importance were transacted there.  As

early as 1735, Philip Lightfoot, a Yorktown merchant, des-

cribed attending the James City County Court in Williamsburg

---

32.  Ibid., November 26, 1772.  Virginia Gazette (Rind),
November 26, 1772.  On the committee, there were four from
Norfolk; three from Petersburg; two each from Yorktown,
Suffolk, Hanover Town, and the Eastern Shore; and one each
from Falmouth, Nansemond, Colchester, Wicomico, Hobb's
Hole, Leedstown, Aylett's, Dumfries, Osborne's, Rocky Ridge,
Hampton, Mattox Bridge, and Williamsburg.

33.  Coulter, "Virginia Merchant," pp. 52-54.  For ex-
ample, Francis Jerdone travelled from his store in Louisa
County to Hanover County Court in July and August, 1757;
to King William Court in January, 1756; and to New Kent
County Court in May, 1756, August, 1758, and March, 1759.
Letterbooks of Francis Jerdone (College of William and
Mary.)

"to receive a Small bill" for a sum owed him by a New Kent County planter.[34] Francis Jerdone referred in 1741 and again in 1749 to the market for bills of exchange at the time of the General Court sessions in Williamsburg.[35] According to his letterbook, Jerdone travelled to Williamsburg from his base of operations in Louisa County in October, 1756; in April, October, and December, 1757; in April and October, 1758; in April, June, October, and December, 1759; and in April and October, 1760, 1761, and 1762.[36] Since merchants and planters from all areas of the colony were in Williamsburg for court sessions, they could take advantage of the opportunity to settle other affairs.

At the Meeting, many types of business could be transacted. Although there appears to have been little display and sale of manufactured goods, occasional references indicate that some Virginia merchants placed

---

34. Philip Lightfoot to William Bassett, August 21, 1735, Bassett Family Papers (Library of Congress).

35. Francis Jerdone to Neil Buchanan, April 23, 1741, Letterbook of Francis Jerdone, I. Jerdone to William Montgomery, May 12, 1749, "Letterbook of Francis Jerdone," William and Mary Quarterly, 1st ser., XI (1902), 155.

36. Letterbook of Francis Jerdone, 1756-1763, passim. It is possible, of course, that Jerdone attended Meetings at other times, not mentioned in his letters.

orders for European goods during the Meetings.  For example,
a Richmond store wrote to a Glasgow firm in 1757 that "we
have Received, all the goods we Bought and ordered at the
gen[era]l court."[37]  In 1773, a Norfolk merchant advertised
"a large Parcel of KENDALL COTTONS," which had been consigned to him by the English manufacturer.  "Any Person in-
clinable to purchase," the advertiser continued, "will
please to apply to him at the ensuing Meeting in Williamsburg."[38]  A year earlier, a Cabin Point storekeeper advised
that those interested in purchasing "the Remains of a Store"
could see the invoice and inventory of goods at the next
Meeting.[39]

Merchants who exported Virginia iron products
could rely upon placing orders at Williamsburg.  A trader
located near Richmond pointed out to a Philadelphia correspondent in 1773 that "the Merch[an]ts....commonly engage
the several quantities [of iron] they may want from the
Iron Masters who attend there."[40]  Auction sales of

---

37.  Coutts & Crosse to John Glassford, November 16, 1757,
Papers of Neil Jamieson (Library of Congress), I, p. 2.

38.  Virginia Gazette (Purdie & Dixon), August 5, 1773.

39.  Ibid., April 16, 1772.

40.  Robert Pleasants to John Pemberton, October 8, 1773,
Letterbook of Robert Pleasants (College of William and Mary).

imported commodities were held fairly often during Public
Times. For example, in 1759 Charles Steuart sent part of
a shipment of powdered sugar from New York "to
W[illiam]sb[ur]g last court in dec[embe]r. to be sold at
public sale."[41]

Although Williamsburg was not a seaport, shippers
usually could secure cargo space there to most major European ports during Public Times. Ship owners and captains
often attended the Meetings to meet merchants for the "Opportunity to commune on Terms of Freight."[42] Those with
vessels to let on charter also advertised their presence
"during the General Court" in Williamsburg to deal with
shippers.[43] Most Virginia shippers placed their marine insurance directly with underwriters in Britain or in Philadelphia. In 1771, though, a Norfolk businessman opened an
"Ensurance Office" where small shippers could order the required insurance; "those who attend the Courts may pay the

---

41. Charles Steuart to Philip Livingston, February 8,
1759, Letterbook of Charles Steuart (Historical Society of
Pennsylvania), II.

42. Virginia Gazette, February 27, 1752; Virginia Gazette (Purdie & Dixon), July 30, 1772; November 4, 1773;
November 11, 1773.

43. Virginia Gazette, October 12, 1752; Virginia Gazette (Purdie & Dixon), June 11, 1767; October 22, 1767;
November 5, 1767.

Premiums" in Williamsburg.[44]

Businessmen could confer at the Meetings regarding the prospective joint ventures of a speculative
nature, such as the slave trade. "In Consequence of the
Conversation we had with you here," began one contract
drawn up by Neil Jamieson and five other merchants in
Williamsburg in May, 1770, "we hereby agree with you to be
each of us concerned in the purchase of a Cargo of Negros
to be made in the West Indies."[45]

The Williamsburg Meetings of Merchants assumed
important functions in the marketing of agricultural exports. Williamsburg was not an assembly and transshipment
point for Virginia's export commodities. Rather, it was
in the mobilization of available information about crops
and prices over a wide area that the Meetings at the provincial capital created "the one central market" in

---

44. _Virginia Gazette_ (Purdie & Dixon), November 14, 1771.

45. Agreement signed by Neil Jamieson, Robert Donald,
John Esdale, Neill Campbell, James Lyle, and James Buchanan,
May 9, 1770, Papers of Neil Jamieson, XII, p. 2551. The
agreement went on to specify prices to be paid for the
slaves in the West Indies, arrangements for insurance and
commissions, methods of sale in Virginia, and the division
of the profits. Jamieson was in charge of the venture.
All of the others operated stores in the Richmond area.
_Virginia Gazette_ (Purdie & Dixon), November 8, 1770; January 10, 1771; June 13, 1771; _Virginia Gazette_ (Rind),
December 1, 1768.

Virginia.[46]

Most fundamental in the economic role of Williamsburg was the growth of the periodic Meeting of Merchants as
an informal clearinghouse for much of the business of Virginia. Since most financial settlements involved foreign
trade in some way, the clearing of intra-Virginia credits
was directly connected with the market for foreign exchange.
And the Meetings in Williamsburg apparently provided the
only active market in Virginia for sterling exchange. As
merchant Charles Steuart pointed out in 1761, "we seldom
can purchase any [bills of exchange] between ye co[ur]ts."[47]

To summarize briefly, the Williamsburg Meeting
of Merchants was an institution which developed to meet the
needs of business for some kind of central system of exchange in a decentralized economy. At these Meetings, merchants performed many business functions ordinarily handled
in a metropolitan center. The Meeting provided the nearest
thing to a commodity market for Virginia's agricultural exports and a money market to mobilize the colony's financial

---

46.   Coulter, "The Virginia Merchant", p. 52.

47.   Charles Steuart to James Wellford, June 30, 1761,
Letterbook of Charles Steuart (Historical Society of Pennsylvania), I.

resources.  The following chapters deal successively with the subjects of marketing agricultural commodities and the financial system, in order that the role of Williamsburg may be seen in clear perspective against the background of Virginia's economic life.

II


THE MARKETING OF AGRICULTURAL COMMODITIES FOR EXPORT


In the words of present-day social scientists, colonial Virginia was an underdeveloped area. Not only was
the Old Dominion a political colony, subject to outside
governmental authority, but it was also a colonial economy -
a region which was economically dependent because of its
specialization on the production of raw materials for export and its reliance on the outside world for most of its
manufactured goods, commercial services, and capital for
economic development.

The purpose of this chapter is to outline the organization of the marketing machinery constructed to collect
Virginia commodities for export and to distribute imported
goods. Far from being parasites, as producers of agricultural commodities often assumed them to be, the merchants
performed the essential task of middlemen in moving goods
and commodities "from where they are wanted less to where

they are wanted more."[1]  Specifically, the marketing machinery constructed by British and Virginia businessmen moved
tobacco and other products from Virginia to European and
West Indian markets, and consumer and capital goods to the
province.

Also to be noted is the role of Williamsburg in
the organization of the colony's trade in agricultural staples.  As indicated earlier, the periodic Meetings of Merchants in the provincial capital served to provide access
to the available information about the state of markets.


## A.   THE TOBACCO TRADE

Tobacco was "King" in colonial Virginia.  Other
economic activities, particularly grain production, grew in
relative importance from the mid-eighteenth century.  But
tobacco still accounted for over three-quarters of the value
of the colony's exports in the 1770's, as indicated in Table I.

That Virginia was truly a colony "built upon smoke"
is demonstrated by the tremendous expansion of tobacco exports, from 20,000 pounds in 1619 to nearly 20,000,000 pounds

---

1.  Abba P. Lerner, "The Myth of the Parasitic Middleman,"
Commentary, VIII (1949), 45-46.

less than a century later. Further growth of tobacco production, particularly from the 1720's, resulted from the
settlement of the Piedmont. By the eve of the American
Revolution, Virginia was exporting between 80,000,000 and
90,000,000 pounds of tobacco each year.[2] An integral part
of this growth process was periodic overproduction, resulting in severe price depressions, as productive capacity
exceeded demand from time to time. But solutions to this
problem could be achieved only as the taste for tobacco became more widespread and British merchants tapped new markets.[3]

Tobacco Production. The two principal varieties
of tobacco were sweet-scented and Oronoko. The former, grown

---

2. Based on data in Table IV, showing imports of tobacco into England and Scotland. Virginia and Maryland together accounted for over 98 per cent of tobacco imports.
Although exact data are not available, Virginia was responsible by the 1760's for the largest share exported from
the two colonies. For Scotland, "the ratio of the Virginia
to the Maryland imports at this time [1773] was generally
three to one or four to one." Jacob Price, "The Rise of
Glasgow in the Chesapeake Tobacco Trade, 1707-1775," William and Mary Quarterly, 3d ser., XI (1954), 195, n. 68.

3. See L. C. Gray, "The Market Surplus Problems of Colonial Tobacco," Agricultural History, II (1928), 1-34;
and Robert P. Thomson, "The Merchant in Virginia, 1700-1775"
(unpublished Ph.D. dissertation, University of Wisconsin,
1955), pp. 51-52.

TABLE I: ESTIMATED VALUES OF THE PRINCIPAL EXPORT COMMOD-
ITIES OF VIRGINIA AND MARYLAND [1773 OR 1774]

| | |
|---|---:|
| Tobacco, 96,000 hogsheads, at 8£ | £ 768,000 |
| Indian corn, beans, pease, &c. | 30,000 |
| Wheat, 40,000 quarters, at 20 s | 40,000 |
| Deer and other skins | 25,000 |
| Iron in bars and pigs | 35,000 |
| Sassafras, snake-root, ginseng, &c. | 7,000 |
| Masts, plank, staves, turpentine, and tar | 55,000 |
| Flax-seed, 7,000 hogsheads, at 40 s. | 14,000 |
| Pickled pork, beef, hams, and bacon | 15,000 |
| Ships built for sale, 30 at 1,000 £ | 30,000 |
| Hemp 1,000 tons at 21 £ | 21,000 |
| | |
| TOTAL | £1,040,000 |

Source: Harry J. Carman, ed., American Husbandry (New York:
Columbia University Press, 1939), p. 183. This
anonymous work was originally published in 1775.

TABLE II:  A RECAPITULATION OF THE QUANTITY OF TOBACCO EX-
PORTED FROM VIRGINIA, SPECIFIED YEARS, 1619-1758

| Year | Crop (in Pounds) |
|------|------------------|
| 1619 | 20,000 |
| 1620 | 40,000 |
| 1621 | 55,000 |
| 1622 | 60,000 |
| 1628 | 500,000 |
| 1639 | 1,500,000 |
| 1640 | 1,300,000 |
| 1641 | 1,300,000 |
| 1688 | 18,157,000 |
| 1704 | 18,295,000 |
| 1745 | 38,232,900 |
| 1746 | 36,217,800 |
| 1747 | 37,623,600 |
| 1748 | 42,104,700 |
| 1749 | 43,188,300 |
| 1750 | 43,710,300 |
| 1751 | 42,032,700 |
| 1752 | 43,542,000 |
| 1753 | 53,862,300 |
| 1754 | 45,722,700 |
| 1755 | 42,918,300 |
| 1756 | 25,606,800 |
| 1757 | short crop |
| 1758 | 22,050,000 |

Source:  Robert A. Brock, "Succinct Account of Tobacco in
Virginia," in J. B. Killebrew, comp., Report on
the Culture and Curing of Tobacco (United States
Census, 1880, III, Agriculture), p. 224.

TABLE III:   NUMBER OF HOGSHEADS OF TOBACCO EXPORTED FROM
             VIRGINIA 1745-1756, 1768-1769, and 1773

| | Upper James | Lower James | York | Rappa-hannock | South Potomac | Total |
|---|---|---|---|---|---|---|
| 1745 | 10,991 | 1,381 | 11,118 | 12,332 | 6,659 | 42,481 |
| 1746 | 10,799 | 1,372 | 11,015 | 10,745 | 6,311 | 40,242 |
| 1747 | 9,355 | 1,718 | 12,895 | 12,132 | 5,704 | 41,804 |
| 1748 | 12,439 | 3,170 | 11,089 | 13,052 | 6,983 | 46,783 |
| 1749 | 11,509 | 3,150 | 10,970 | 15,012 | 7,346 | 47,987 |
| 1750 | 12,974 | 2,218 | 13,802 | 14,331 | 5,242 | 48,567 |
| 1751 | 10,858 | 2,525 | 12,054 | 13,553 | 7,713 | 46,703 |
| 1752 | 13,530 | 1,423 | 12,623 | 14,299 | 6,505 | 48,380 |
| 1753 | 18,830 | 2,113 | 15,127 | 16,815 | 6,959 | 59,847[c] |
| 1754 | 13,900 | 1,131 | 14,878 | 13,512 | 7,332 | 50,803 |
| 1755 | 13,739 | 918 | 15,344 | 11,963 | 5,723 | 47,687 |
| 1756 | 7,262 | 1,096 | 6,918 | 8,531 | 4,645 | 28,452 |
| 1768[a] | 15,860 | 1,504 | 5,668 | 9,105 | 5,512 | 39,623[d] |
| 1769[a] | 17,825 | 1,993 | 8,225 | 9,920 | 9,143 | 50,222[e] |
| 1772[a] | 24,900[b] | ----- | 8,634 | 14,549 | 10,716 | 65,208[f] |
| 1773[a] | 27,592 | 4,674 | 8,248 | 13,244 | 10,541 | 69,587[g] |

a  Crop year, from October 1 of previous year to October 1 of
   year indicated.
b  Includes Lower James District also.
c  Includes 3 hogsheads exported from Accomack District.
d  Includes 1,974 hogsheads exported in "free bottoms," or
   ships registered in Virginia.  See Hening, Statutes,
   Vol. VIII, p. 252.
e  Includes 3,116 hogsheads exported in "free bottoms."
f  Includes 6,409 hogsheads exported in "free bottoms."
g  Includes 5,288 hogsheads exported in "free bottoms."

Source:   1745-1756, Edward D. Neill, The Fairfaxes of Eng-
          land and America in the Seventeenth and Eighteenth
          Centuries (Albany, N. Y.: Joel Munsell, 1868),
          p. 225

          1768, Jerman Baker to Thomas Adams, January 8,
          1769, Adams Papers (Virginia Historical Society).

          1769, Virginia Gazette (Rind), November 2, 1769.

          1772, Virginia Gazette (Purdie & Dixon), November 19,
          1772.

          1773, Ibid., November 11, 1773.

TABLE IV:    IMPORTS OF TOBACCO, ENGLAND AND SCOTLAND, 1761-1775.

| Date | England (pounds) | Scotland (pounds) | Total |
|------|------------------|-------------------|-------|
| 1761 | 47,065,787 | 24,048,380 | 71,114,167 |
| 1762 | 44,102,491 | 27,339,433 | 71,441,924 |
| 1763 | 65,173,752 | 31,613,170 | 96,786,922 |
| 1764 | 54,433,318 | 26,310,219 | 80,743,537 |
| 1765 | 48,306,593 | 33,889,565 | 82,196,158 |
| 1766 | 43,307,453 | 32,175,223 | 75,482,676 |
| 1767 | 39,140,639 | 29,385,343 | 68,525,982 |
| 1768 | 35,545,708 | 33,261,427 | 68,807,135 |
| 1769 | 33,784,208 | 35,920,685 | 69,704,893 |
| 1770 | 39,187,037 | 39,226,354 | 78,413,391 |
| 1771 | 58,079,183 | 49,312,146 | 107,391,329 |
| 1772 | 51,493,522 | 43,748,415 | 95,241,937 |
| 1773 | 55,928,957 | 44,485,194 | 100,414,151 |
| 1774 | 56,048,393 | 40,457,589 | 106,505,982 |
| 1775 | 55,965,463 | 55,927,542 | 111,893,005 |

Source: Lewis C. Gray, History of Agriculture in the Southern United States to 1860 (New York: Peter Smith, 1941), I, 214.   Data were compiled from customhouse records by David Macpherson, Annals of Commerce, Manufactures, Fisheries, and Navigation...(London, 1805), III, 583.

principally in the sandy loams of the peninsula between the
James and York, was distinguished by its round leaf, fine
fibers, and mild flavor.  Oronoko was coarser, bulkier,
and stronger in flavor, and its production more widely distributed through the tobacco-growing areas of the colony.
Sweet-scented, which commanded a premium in English markets
during much of the seventeenth century, was gradually dis-
placed during the eighteenth century by better grades of
Oronoko.  Although several subvarieties of the latter
were recognized, almost all tobacco was officially classi-
fied simply as Oronoko by the latter part of the eighteenth
century.[4]

The quality and quantity of tobacco produced on
any plantation depended upon two factors: the type and condition of the soil and the care with which the planter cultivated and prepared his tobacco for market.  According to
an eighteenth-century authority,

---

4.  Lewis C. Gray, History of Agriculture in the Southern United States to 1860 (New York: Peter Smith, 1941),
I, 217-218.  Arthur P. Middleton, Tobacco Coast:  A Maritime History of Chesapeake Bay in the Colonial Era (Newport News: The Mariners' Museum, 1953), pp. 97-98.  In addition to the data on exports of tobacco included in the
tables in this chapter and the appendix, see the statistics in U. S. Bureau of the Census, Historical Statistics
of the United States, Colonial Times to 1957 (Washington,
D. C.: Government Printing Office, 1960), series Z 223-253,
pp. 765-767.

the lands which are found to answer best, in
their natural state in Virginia, are the light
red, or chocolate coloured mountain lands; the
light black mountain soil in the coves of the
mountains, and the richest low grounds. Hence
has arisen the general reputation of the Virginia tobaccos, and, chiefly, the local repu-
tations of particular tobaccos brought to
market: as, for example, James's River tobacco, Tayloe's Mountain Quarter tobacco,
&c. which are preferred.[5]

Since "a Virginian never thinks of reinstating

or manuring his land until he can find no more land," the

exhausting nature of tobacco cultivation generally required

abandonment in three or four years. Exhausted land returned

to timber regained some of its fertility in twenty years

or so, but it was less productive than new lands.[6] One

planter among many who were looking to the mountain area

for fresh tobacco land reported in 1771 that those "who

have moved from Gloster to Frederick make near 5 times as

much as they did down here."[7] Tobacco produced on new land

---

5. William Tatham, An Historical and Practical Essay
on the Culture and Commerce of Tobacco (London: Vernor &
Hood, 1800), pp. 5-6. See also Avery O. Craven, Soil Exhaustion as a Factor in the Agricultural History of Virginia and Maryland, 1606-1860 (Urbana: University of Illinois, 1926), p. 61.

6. Craven, Soil Exhaustion, p. 69. Tatham, Essay on
Tobacco, p. 6.

7. John Page, Jr. to John Norton & Son, October 11,
1771, Frances N. Mason, ed., John Norton & Sons: Merchants
of London and Virginia (Richmond: Dietz Press, 1937), p. 199.

was likely to be of better quality than that from a previously worked tract; this was implied by a planter who insisted to a London merchant that his tobacco was "made at my Plantation in Brunswick on fresh Land."[8]

Equally important in producing tobacco of good quality was the method of cultivation, which consisted of a series of tasks which required painstaking care. Each of the processes - seed-planting, transplanting, topping, suckering, worming, and cutting - had to be undertaken at a proper time of growth under precise weather conditions. During preparation for market - curing, stripping, stemming, and prizing into hogsheads - only long experience could determine whether the plant was in case for the next operation, that is, "in a condition which will bear handling and stripping, without either being so dry as to break and crumble, or so damp as to endanger a future rotting of the leaf." No profit would be derived by the planter who "should blunder in this one point only, then wanted to complete a marketable staple, and become thus involved in a total loss of his whole crop, and have the expences to pay into the bargain,

---

8. Moses Robertson to John Norton & Son, September 21, 1772, ibid., p. 274.

for bringing an unmerchantable article to market."[9]

Buyers usually were willing to pay a premium for quantities of tobacco cultivated by men of experience and good reputation who worked good lands.  This tobacco was then expected to yield a premium in English markets, as indicated by this comment of an early eighteenth-century tobacco buyer to his English correspondent:

> I must make bold to mention a great Evil that I
> think to be in ye Tob[acc]o. Trade which is in
> Selling a several persons Tobo. Together to one
> Man So y[a]t. if mine is never so good beyond the
> rest I shall have no more for it, than he that owns
> ye meanest sort in that parcell Altho my Tobo. de-
> servs a penny p[er] lb. more.  Therefore earnestly
> desires my Tobo. may be sold it by. Self without
> being lumpt of with others. for I am well Satis-
> fyed (for ye Quantity of it) there is not a better
> parcill of Tobo. Comes from our parts of ye Coun-
> try and I believe not nigh so good I can assure you
> the greatest part of it has cost me above 7 £
> Sterl[ing] p h[ogs]h[ea]d before goeing on Board
> of the Ship Therefore hopes it may come to a good
> Mark[e]t. with You to fetch me so much Money to
> Enable me to give an Encouraging price to those
> that will take Care to make such good Tobo.[10]

In order to improve the quality and the reputation and price of Virginia tobacco, the inspection law of 1730 required that all Tobacco destined for export be brought

---

9.  Tatham, _Essay on Tobacco_, pp. 7-27, 37, 42.

10.  Robert Anderson to Messrs. Micajah Richd Perry, n.d. [written between March-May, 1715], Letterbook of Robert Anderson (University of Virginia).

to public warehouses, located at convenient points on the navigable rivers, generally about twelve to fourteen miles apart. If the public inspectors, two in number at each warehouse after 1732, approved the tobacco as "good, sound, well-conditioned, and merchantable, and free from trash, sand, and dirt," they were to place an official stamp upon the hogshead and issue a certificate to the planter. Trash was to be burned. The tobacco note, which was a title to the tobacco and changed hands when the planter sold or exported the hogsheads, was accepted for payment of taxes and possessed limited negotiability. Crop notes listed specific hogsheads by mark and number, while transfer notes, representing tobacco brought in loose bundles, entitled the bearer to the same quantity and type of tobacco.[11]

In spite of some opposition in the 1730's, inspection proved successful in its goal of removing the poorest grades of tobacco from trade, to the mutual benefit of merchant and planter. Occasionally, inspectors were lax, as

---

11. William W. Hening, ed., The Statutes at Large: being a Collection of All the Laws of Virginia (Richmond, 1810-1823), IV, 247-270. Although earlier attempts had been made to establish an inspection system, this was the first successful statute and remained the basic law, with minor amendments, through the rest of the colonial period. Thomson, "Merchant in Virginia," pp. 95-125.

was pointed out by one merchant to his backcountry store-

keeper in 1772:

> I wish you would discourage your Customers as much
> as you can with prudence from carrying their Tobo.
> to Ozburnes Warehouse [as] that Inspection is under
> a very bad character at present in England, the
> planters goes out of their way to it on Acc[oun]t.
> of its being favourable.[12]

But another merchant was more optimistic, stating that the

inspectors at Aquia on the Potomac "are great villains, but

I hope they will soon be turned out."[13]


   <u>Major Markets</u>.  According to British law, tobacco

was on the list of enumerated commodities, that is, commod-

ities which could be exported only to Britain.  Furthermore,

the Navigation Acts required that tobacco, like all colonial

products, could be exported only in ships which were built,

owned, and manned by British (including British colonial)

subjects.[14]

---

12.  David Ross to John White Holt, August 17, 1772,
John Hook Papers (Duke University).

13.  Harry Piper to Dixon & Littledale, June 15, 1772,
Letterbook of Harry Piper (University of Virginia).

14.  For details of the British system of Mercantilism,
see Lawrence A. Harper, <u>The English Navigation Laws</u> (New
York: Columbia University Press, 1939).  Oliver M. Dickerson,
<u>The Navigation Acts and the American Revolution</u> (Philadelphia:
University of Pennsylvania Press, 1951), Chapters I-III,

By the beginning of the eighteenth century, London had outdistanced all outport competitors to become the major British tobacco market. While Bristol still held an important position as distributor in the domestic market, London in 1720 handled at least two-thirds of the tobacco imported by Great Britain.[15]

However, from the early part of the century, Glasgow began to challenge London's supremacy. The rapid rise of Scotland in the tobacco trade is illustrated in Table V, which shows tobacco imports of Scotland at specified years from 1707 to 1775. Scotland's relative growth was even more striking. As late as 1738, the Scottish ports accounted for only ten per cent of total British imports of tobacco. This rose to 20 per cent in 1744, 30 per cent in 1758, 40 per cent in 1765, and almost 52 per cent in 1769, declining slightly to 45 per cent on the eve of the American Revolution.[16] By the last decade of the colonial period, London

---

contain the most recent interpretation of the effects of the laws upon economic life and development in the colonies.

15. Middleton, Tobacco Coast, p. 110. For details of Bristol's role in the tobacco trade in the 1720's, see Walter E. Minchinton, "The Virginia Letters of Isaac Hobhouse, Merchant of Bristol," Virginia Magazine of History and Biography, LXVI (1958), 278-301.

16. Price, "Glasgow in the Chesapeake Tobacco Trade," pp. 180-181.

was a distant second as a destination of Virginia tobacco,
as evidenced by the data on exports from the Upper James
Naval District shown in Table VI.

As Professor Price has pointed out, the Scots possessed several advantages, once the Act of Union of 1707
removed the legal disabilities of Scottish trade with the
colonies by placing Scotland within the closed commercial
system of Britain.  For one thing, the route to Virginia
from Glasgow was safer and shorter than that from London.
Liverpool and Whitehaven also took advantage of this route
to expand their colonial trade.  More important, though,
were the capital resources supplied by the Glasgow banks
which specialized in mobilizing credit for the tobacco trade.
Equally significant was the Scottish business efficiency,
which brought lower operating costs than those of the Lon-
doners, particularly in reducing the turn-around time of
ships in Virginia.  Fundamental to the increased activity
of the Scots was their tapping of the trade of the expanding
Piedmont with their establishment of the store system to purchase tobacco and sell goods, a subject to be treated in ensuing pages.  Finally, Glasgow's continued growth after mid-
century can be seen as part of "a tendency towards specialization among the outports: Bristol in the West India Trade,

TABLE V:   TOBACCO IMPORTS, SCOTLAND, SPECIFIED YEARS, 1708-
           1771.

| Year | Amount (Pounds) |
|------|-----------------|
| 1708 | 1,450,000 |
| 1715 | 2,500,000 |
| 1722 | 6,000,000 |
| 1741 | 8,000,000 |
| 1743 | 10,000,000 |
| 1745 | 13,000,000 |
| 1752 | 21,000,000 |
| 1753 | 24,000,000 |
| 1760 | 32,000,000 |
| 1771 | 47,000,000 |

Source:   Jacob M. Price, "The Rise of Glasgow in the Chesa-
          peake Tobacco Trade, 1707-1775," William and Mary
          Quarterly, 3d ser., XI, (1954), 180.  Data are
          from T. 1/139/29, C. O. 390/5/13, T. 1/282/23, T.
          36/13, T. 1/329 fol. 125, Customs 14, Public Record
          Office.


TABLE VI:   DESTINATION OF TOBACCO EXPORTS, UPPER DISTRICT
            OF JAMES RIVER, OCTOBER 25, 1765 - OCTOBER 25,
            1766

| Destination | Hogsheads |
|-------------|-----------|
| London | 2,470 |
| Bristol | 1,493 |
| Liverpool | 1,730 |
| Whitehaven | 1,877 |
| Hull | 165 |
| Penryn | 404 |
| Falmouth | 95 |
| Scotland | 11,176 |
| Total | 19,410 |

Source:   Virginia Gazette (Purdie & Dixon), January 22, 1767.

TABLE VII:   TOBACCO EXPORTS, ENGLAND AND SCOTLAND, 1773

| | England | Scotland | Total |
|---|---|---|---|
| | | (Pounds) | |
| Africa | 990,873 | -------- | 990,873 |
| Denmark & Norway | 2,573,284 | 812,650 | 3,385,934 |
| East Country | 265,019 | -------- | 265,019 |
| East Indies | 53,915 | -------- | 53,915 |
| Flanders | 7,150,737 | -------- | 7,150,737 |
| France | 7,343,883 | 24,406,240 | 31,750,123 |
| Germany | 11,953,577 | 1,982,347 | 13,935,924 |
| Greenland | 1,521 | -------- | 1,521 |
| Holland | 14,371,835 | 14,629,050 | 29,000,885 |
| Ireland | 1,855,923 | 4,333,850 | 6,189,773 |
| Italy | 1,378,156 | -------- | 1,378,156 |
| Madeira | 100 | -------- | 100 |
| Russia | 22,048 | -------- | 22,048 |
| Spain | 229,722 | -------- | 229,722 |
| Sweden | 1,076,078 | -------- | 1,076,078 |
| Venice | 25,209 | -------- | 25,209 |
| Channel Islands | 825,111 | -------- | 825,111 |
| North America | 170,510 | 48,446 | 218,856 |
| West Indies | 94,474 | 25,355 | 119,829 |
| | | | |
| Total | 50,386,925 | 46,389,518 | 96,776,443 |
| | [50,381,975] | [46,237,938] | [96,619,913] |

Source:   Adam Anderson, Historical and Chronological Deduction of the Origin of Commerce, revised by Mr.
Coombe (Dublin: P. Byrne, 1790), VI, 599.   Totals
in source were incorrect.   Totals in brackets are
corrected figures.

Liverpool in the slave trade, Glasgow in the tobacco trade."[17]

From the mid-seventeenth century, when the demand for tobacco in England began to level off, Continental markets expanded to keep pace with the rising production in English America. By the mid-eighteenth century, the Chesapeake colonies were supplying tobacco to all of Europe. Indeed, about 90 per cent of the total tobacco imports of England and Scotland were reexported in the five years 1770-1774.[18]

Table VII shows the leading European customers for British tobacco in 1772. Although Amsterdam was an important processing and distributing center for all the Continent in the seventeenth century, European buyers more generally by-passed the Amsterdam market to purchase their tobacco directly in London or Glasgow in the eighteenth century.[19]

---

17. Ibid., pp. 183-191

18. Gray, Agriculture in the Southern United States to 1860, I, 255. Middleton, Tobacco Coast, pp. 126-127.

19. Violet Barbour, Capitalism in Amsterdam in the Seventeenth Century (Baltimore: Johns Hopkins Press, 1950), pp. 63, 93-94. Vertrees J. Wyckoff, Tobacco Regulation in Colonial Maryland (Baltimore: Johns Hopkins Press, 1936), p. 116. Gray, Agriculture in the Southern United States to 1860, I, 254-255. Price, "Glasgow in the Chesapeake Tobacco Trade," pp. 190-191. Jacob M. Price, The Tobacco Adventure to Russia: Enterprise, Politics, and Diplomacy in the Quest for a Northern Market for English Colonial

The French played a most important role in the British tobacco market during the eighteenth century, taking in some
years nearly one-half of British exports of the commodity.
Because tobacco was a government monopoly in France, the
agent of the French Farmers General of the Revenue had considerable bargaining power in dealing with the many English
and Scottish merchants.  Through the use of shrewd market
tactics, such as purchasing "successively, and in small
Parcels" and playing London against the outports, the
French buyer was able at times to control the price to his
advantage.  Attempts were made in the 1720's and again in
the 1730's to introduce a scheme of direct purchase of tobacco in the colonies for the French, but London merchants
successfully defeated the proposal, in spite of the conten-
tion by proponents of the plan that economies in marketing
would reduce the price to the French and at the same time
increase the profits of the colonial producer and the British
trader.[20]

---

Tobacco, Transactions of the American Philosophical Society,
new ser., vol. 51, pt. 1 (Philadelphia, 1961), 101-103, con-
tains data on volume of tobacco exports to northern Europe.

    20.  Middleton, Tobacco Coast, pp. 129-130.  Gray points
out that the trade with France was so important that, during
the War of the Austrian Succession and the Seven Years' War,
the belligerents issued special passes exempting from capture
British or neutral vessels carrying tobacco from Britain to

The Marketing Mechanism: The Consignment System.

When tobacco was ready for shipment, there were two principal

methods of marketing: the consignment system and the direct

purchase system.

Those using the consignment method shipped their

tobacco to a British merchant who supervised the unloading,

paid the customs duties, carted the tobacco to warehouses,

and sold the commodity at the best market price. For these

services the British consignment merchant generally received

2 1/2 per cent of the gross sales. In addition, he attended

to many other needs of the planter - providing transpor-

tation, securing insurance, and supervising the purchase

of goods. Each year the account current was prepared,

showing net sales of tobacco after expenses were deducted,

and the cost of goods ordered by the planter.[21] The Vir-

ginia consignor bore the risks and expenses of transpor-

tation and marketing, but the British merchant provided the

---

France. Agriculture in the Southern United States to 1860,
I, 255. See Jacob M. Price, "The French Farmers-General
in the Chesapeake: The MacKercher-Huber Mission of 1737-1738,"
William and Mary Quarterly, 3d ser., XIV (1957), 125-153,
for an account of one plan to promote direct trade with
France.

21. Thomson, "Merchant in Virginia," Chapter II. See

financing.  In 1769, for example, John Norton & Sons of
London employed a capital of £6,000 plus £12,000 of borrowed funds in the sale of 741 hogsheads consigned to them.[22]

Much of the consignment business was centered in
London, although the outports continued to participate in
the trade through the colonial period.  But limiting the
volume of business which any individual merchant could
handle, was the personal attention demanded by each customer.
When George Norton increased shipments to his father's firm
in 1774, William Reynolds wrote to him that too much tobacco consigned to his father "must necessarily prevent his
paying that particular attention a Man might do with 5 or
600 h[ogs]h[ead]s."[23]

In Virginia, many of the large planters, who were
the most prevalent consignors, consigned not only tobacco
produced on their own plantations but also tobacco purchased
from small planters and farmers.  There were also merchants

---

Mason, John Norton & Sons, for correspondence regarding
many of the details of the consignment system.

22.  John Norton to [John Hatley Norton], April 21, 1770,
ibid., pp. 129-130.

23.  William Reynolds to George F. Norton, June 3, 1774,
Letterbook of William Reynolds (Library of Congress), I.

like Robert Anderson in the early eighteenth century who purchased tobacco for consignment.[24]

In most cases, the commission merchant maintained an agent or employee in Virginia to solicit consignments. John Hatley Norton, first acting as agent for his father and then serving as junior partner, spent many days "riding Journeys in such a hot Country, [which] must be very fatiguing."[25] Ship captains, too, travelled around the county courts to contact prospective customers. When the English firm did not have its own full-time agent in the colony, it usually retained the services of a Virginia merchant to supervise its business in the colony, particularly the collection of debts. The normal commission for settling accounts and making remittances appears to have been 5 per cent, but Charles Steuart offered in 1751 to transact business for Bowden & Farquhar of London for 2 1/2 per cent.[26]

---

24. See Letterbook of Robert Anderson, passim.

25. See Turner to [John Hatley Norton], March 27, 1768, in Mason, John Norton & Sons, p. 40.

26. Charles Steuart to Bowden & Farquhar, July 20, 1751, Letterbook of Charles Steuart (Historical Society of Pennsylvania), I.

The most important benefits derived by the consigning planter were the realization of the full market price for tobacco in England and the credit for necessary imported goods. The system, though, rested on mutual trust: that the merchant sold the consignment of tobacco for the best market price and that the planter shipped tobacco in sufficient quantities to cover the cost of the goods which he ordered from England. Many consignors undoubtedly were well satisfied that their English correspondents exerted every effort on their behalf, as in the case of one Virginian who wrote: "I have lost considerably by my last Consignment of Tob[acc]o, but this I know you could not help."[27] Considerable understanding of rapidly fluctuating markets in Britain was necessary for this comment:

> You seem to be uneasy, that you shall not be able
> to render as good an Acc[oun]t. of Sales for the
> Tob[acc]o. of last Year as you did for that of
> the preceeding; but all reasonable Men will make
> Allowance for the Difference of Circumstances, and
> the unreasonable are not to be satisfied with any
> Thing.[28]

However, all tobacco growers were not reasonable,

---

27. R. C. Nicholas to [John Norton], November 30, 1772, Mason, John Norton & Sons, p. 283.

28. William Nelson to John Norton, August 11, 1772, ibid., p. 268.

and it was inevitable that the great distance between merchant and planter would result in some misunderstanding.
Some Virginians complained about lack of care in transacting
business, as did Robert Anderson in the early eighteenth century:

> I find by your Measures to me that my Concerns is
> not worth Your minding, for I have not been used
> to be obliged to go to other Men to Know my Af-
> fairs till being Concerned with you and I was in
> hopes your Principles did not allow makeing such
> differences in Respect to Persons but since I
> find it is so I desire you to Settle my Acc[oun]t.[29]

At times, the ship captain was guilty of an oversight in
loading tobacco. The master of one of John Norton's ships
was the target of this criticism:

> I had advised you in my last that I had shipt you
> six H[ogs]h[ea]ds of Tobacco, and I had actually
> delivered orders for them, but I find Robinson
> was kind enough to leave them out, and he has
> treated Mrs. Chamberlayne in the same manner. I
> think it strange that your particular Friends
> should be thus treated, many others complain and
> I wish it may not hurt your interest with them.[30]

Many complaints were directed to what the planter
regarded as excessive selling charges. The nominal commission of 2 1/2 per cent of gross sales actually amounted

---

29.  Robert Anderson to Gilbert Higginson, May 11, 1715,
Letterbook of Robert Anderson.

30.  Petr Lyons to John Norton, November 20, 1771, Mason,
John Norton & Sons, p. 207.

to as much as 8 to 10 per cent of the net proceeds, since

the commission was levied against all charges and duties.

Fixed charges - freight, insurance, primage, wharfage, por-

terage, lighterage, storage, and customs duties - generally

amounted to 75 to 90 per cent of the price to the consumer

but sometimes resulted in a loss to the producer. Because

these charges varied little whether tobacco prices were

high or low, a small percentage change in consumer prices,

when shifted back to the producer, made a comparatively

large percentage difference in prices received.[31]

Endless controversies developed over the prices

and quality of goods ordered by the planters. If prices

were higher than anticipated, or the condition and quality

less than perfect, or the goods ordered not precisely what

the planter had in mind (whether or not his specifications

had been precise), the commission merchant was blamed.[32]

---

31.  Gray, Southern Agriculture in the United States to
1860, I, 275.  Thomson, "Merchant in Virginia," p. 49.  Primage is an allowance paid by the consignee to the mariners
and master of a vessel for loading the cargo.  Porterage is
an allowance paid porters for carrying the goods away from
the wharf, or for shipping them from the wharf.  Wharfage
is the fee paid for landing goods on a wharf, or for shipping
them from the wharf.  Lighterage is the fee paid for transporting the cargo from the ship to the wharf.  Thomson,
"Merchant in Virginia," p. 38, n. 19.

32.  See, for example, Rebecca Chamberlayne to John

On the other side, planters were sometimes guilty of overextending their accounts, either by drawing bills of exchange against the proceeds of future shipments or extravagent orders of goods. Indeed, some expected large advances as a condition of consignment to a particular merchant, as one Virginian observed in the 1770's:

Some people are so very unreasonable in their Expectations to have Money advanced, that it is extremely difficult to avoid giving them Umbrage. The Misfortune is that, if one Merch[an]t. will not comply with their Desires, they fly to another.[33]

Many of these charges levied by planters and by merchants were valid, but both groups of participants in the consignment derived benefits. The trade was highly profitable to the merchant who managed it properly, as a recent study of the operations of John Norton & Son has demonstrated, and from the London businessman the planter received the necessary services of a banker and merchandizing agent. At its best, the consignment system was

---

Norton, July 13, 1771; Petr. Lyons to John Norton, July 15, 1771; R. C. Nicholas to [John Norton], September 7, 1771, Mason, John Norton & Sons, pp. 165-166, 168, 184. Actually, much of the irritation conveyed in these letters was directed against the London tradesmen, but Virginians urged more careful supervision by Norton.

33. R. C. Nicholas to John Norton & Sons, July 30, 1773, ibid., p. 341. On the extravagent buying habits of planters, see Emory G. Evans, "Planter Indebtedness and the

"rooted in friendship and mutual trust between planter and merchant" and "worked fairly well to bring to both parties the benefits of trade."[34]

The consignment system was used extensively in the seventeenth and early eighteenth centuries, but it was to be supplemented and eventually surpassed by an alternative marketing system - the direct purchase of tobacco in the colony. By the eve of the American Revolution, shipments by planters to English merchants accounted for a relatively small share of Virginia's tobacco exports, perhaps as little as one-quarter.[35] James Parker, Norfolk merchant, may have exaggerated in 1770 that "the trade of Consigning Tob[acco] to the London Merch[an]ts seems to be nearly at an end,"[36] but shipments by planters comprised less than 15 per cent of the exports of tobacco from the Upper James

---

Coming of the Revolution in Virginia," _William and Mary Quarterly_, 3d ser., XIX (1962), 518-519.

34. Samuel M. Rosenblatt, "The Significance of Credit in the Tobacco Consignment Trade: A Study of John Norton & Sons, 1768-1775," _William and Mary Quarterly_, 3d ser., XIX (1962), 383-399.

35. Middleton, _Tobacco Coast_, p. 110.

36. James Parker to Charles Steuart, January 28, 1770, Charles Steuart Papers (National Library of Scotland), MS. 5040, p. 81.

naval district in 1773-1775.[37]


### The Marketing Mechanism: The Direct Purchase of Tobacco.

Under the direct purchase method, in contrast to consignment, title to the tobacco passed from the producer to the resident agent or employee of a British firm. The latter assumed the responsibility and risk of shipping and marketing.

This marketing mechanism developed in response to two forces in eighteenth-century Virginia - the settlement of the Piedmont region and the entry of the Scottish merchants into the tobacco trade. The first stimulated a tremendous expansion of tobacco production and created new marketing problems, since ocean-going ships could not navigate into the region above the fall line. However, London merchants, who controlled much of the consignment trade of the Tidewater, were reluctant to pursue vigorously the business of this new area. Into this situation stepped the Scottish traders to take advantage of a potentially lucrative commerce.[38]

---

37. Robert P. Thomson, "The Tobacco Export of the Upper James River Naval District, 1773-1775," William and Mary Quarterly, 3d ser., XVIII (1961), 400.

38. Price, "Glasgow in the Chesapeake Tobacco Trade,"

The innovation of the Glasgow traders was the store system, which made it possible to serve the small planters and farmers of the backcountry. These small-scale tobacco producers could not bear the risks of the consignment system. Also, merchants 3,000 miles away could not readily assess the credit standing of many small customers, although storekeepers in the neighborhood might be able to assess the risks of dealing with individual planters and farmers.[39] Furthermore, the adoption of the inspection system in 1730, establishing a minimum standard of quality and providing a simple method of transferring title to un-differentiated tobacco, encouraged Scottish businessmen to entrust the purchase of tobacco to factors and employees.[40]

Many of the early Scottish traders in Virginia were travelling merchants. Each venture of the "Scots peddlars," as they were called, appears to have been financed and organized separately by a group of merchants, who

pp. 183-191. Thomson, "Merchant in Virginia," pp. 157-168.

39. Jacob M. Price, "The French Market for Chesapeake Tobacco, 1730-1775" (paper delivered at the Conference on Early American History, Charlottesville, Virginia, October, 1960).

40. Richard Pares, Merchants and Planters, Economic History Review Supplement 4 (Cambridge: Cambridge University Press, 1960), p. 36.

appointed one of their number as supercargo to supervise the sale of goods and the purchase of tobacco.[41]

Within a few decades after their entry into the trade, a more permanent organization was in operation. Resident factors[42] established stores at likely locations, particularly in the small communities which grew up at the fall line, or those around the tobacco warehouses along the rivers, or others at the courthouses of the new Piedmont counties.[43] These agents received a commission, usually of five per cent on tobacco purchased and ten per cent on imported goods sold.[44] Some, like Francis Jerdone of Louisa County, also engaged on their own accounts in other types of business, such as the West India trade; sometimes, they speculated in consignments

---

41. H. R. Fox Bourne, English Merchants: Memoirs in Illustration of the Progress of British Commerce (London: Richard Bentley, 1866), II, 179-180.

42. According to an eighteenth-century authority, "a Factor is a Correspondent or Agent residing beyond Seas, or in some remote Part, commissioned by Merchants (called his Employers) to buy or sell Goods for their Account, or some way to assist them in carrying on Commerce." John Mair, Book-keeping Methodiz'd: or a Methodical Treatise of Merchant-Accompts, 2d ed. (Edinburgh: W. Sands, 1741), p. 224.

43. Thomson, "Merchant in Virginia," pp. 175-180.

44. A. F. Voke, "Accounting Methods of Colonial Merchants in Virginia," Journal of Accountancy, XLII (1926), 5.

of tobacco which they purchased.[45]

Furthermore, some English firms developed a business in the direct purchase of tobacco in the colony. For example, Roger Atkinson of Petersburg factored for the Lydes of London, and Harry Piper of Alexandria acted as agent for Dixon & Littledale of Whitehaven.[46]

The Marketing Mechanism: The Williamsburg Meetings of Merchants. Although much of the actual purchase of Virginia tobacco was made at stores and county courts throughout the colony, and although tobacco was shipped directly from public warehouses, the Meetings of Merchants in Williamsburg provided the nearest approach to a central market in the province. Traders and planters, in their bids and offers, helped to disclose the supply and demand situation and thus to establish a price which was of colony-wide significance.[47]

---

45. In 1759, the purchase of a cargo of tobacco, which cost £8,646, earned Jerdone a commission of £432. Invoice of 310 h[ogs]h[ea]ds Tobacco, bought by Francis Jerdone, by order & for acco[un]t of Messrs Alexander Spiers & Hugh Brown Merch[an]ts in Glasgow, June 1st, 1759. Letterbook of Francis Jerdone (College of William and Mary), II.

46. Letterbook of Roger Atkinson and Letterbook of Harry Piper (both in University of Virginia.)

47. One authority has pointed to the market as "a more

Tobacco prices, like those of other agricultural commodities, fluctuated widely. All of the factors affecting supply and demand had to be considered in determining a price which would be paid for each kind of tobacco produced in Virginia. Letters from the colony to Britain contained detailed information on the condition of growing crops and estimates and revisions of estimates of future crops based on changing weather conditions at any particular stage of the crop year. In turn, letters from Britain to Virginia commented on current market conditions and on the prospects for future changes. Seemingly, it should have been a simple matter for the British merchant to set an upper limit at which his factors could purchase tobacco, count on his factors to exercise shrewdness in obtaining tobacco for as much under the limit as possible, dispatch his ships to carry the tobacco to British markets, and then sell his cargoes at a profit. Because communication was so slow and poorly organized, however, information regarding market and crop conditions was always outdated or at least discounted.

---

or less organized group of individuals whose bids and offers disclose the supply and demand situation and thereby establish the price." Charles O. Hardy, "Market," Encyclopaedia of the Social Sciences (New York: Macmillan, 1930-34), X, 131-133.

Since trade in Virginia was decentralized and ultimate markets were far away, the Williamsburg Meetings provided a focal point for pricing decisions. Here all of the available information on market conditions could be assessed. Buyers and sellers could determine over-all crop prospects and compare data on conditions at the major markets in Britain. For example, Francis Jerdone, who purchased tobacco in Louisa County, knew well the crop situation in the area drained by the York River and its tributaries, but from Williamsburg he could report that "by all information I can get here, tobacco is as scarce every where as on York River."[48]

After merchants and planters at the Meetings balanced the probable size and quality of the Virginia crop against the latest advices from Britain, they began to buy and sell a little tobacco. When a price was accepted by any considerable number of buyers and sellers, it was said to be "broke," or to have become the prevailing market price, usually referred to as the "Court price."[49] Whether or not

---

48.   Francis Jerdone to Capt. Robert Craford, April 28, 1758, Letterbook of Francis Jerdone.

49.   Calvin B. Coulter, "The Virginia Merchant" (unpublished Ph.D. dissertation, Princeton University, 1944), pp. 105-106.   Robert Pleasants to Joshua Fischer & Sons,

a large volume of trading was conducted at Williamsburg,
the price established there had considerable significance.
As James Robinson, chief factor of the Cuninghame stores
in the colony, pointed out in 1769, "there will be no certain
price untill we return from the Generall Court."[50]

Certainly, it would be too much to claim the
status of a modern commodity exchange for the Williamsburg
Meeting. It lacked formal organization as well as some of
the special functions normally performed by an exchange,
such as a futures market. Nor did the Meeting satisfy all
of the requirements for a completely efficient market, de-
fined as "standardization of qualities, localization of
transactions, and full knowledge."[51] The inspection system
provided only a minimum quality requirement for tobacco.
More transactions were made outside of Williamsburg than
at the provincial capital, and prices for tobacco varied
in different parts of the colony because of the differences

---

March 12, 1773, Letterbook of Robert Pleasants (College of
William & Mary.)

50. James Robinson to John Turner, April 22, 1769,
Letterbook of William Cuninghame & Company (National Library of Scotland), I.

51. George J. Stigler, The Theory of Price (New York:
Macmillan, 1952), p. 56.

in types of tobacco produced.[52]   Quality varied also among

individual producers, as noted earlier, so that recognized

makers of particularly good leaf received a premium price.[53]

And local conditions, such as the number of ships in one

river, influenced pricing decisions.[54]   But the prices

quoted at Williamsburg were of importance to traders through-

out the colony.   It was in the mobilization of available

information about supply and demand that the Williamsburg

Meeting of Merchants made its contribution to the operation

of the marketing mechanism.


Organization of the Store Trade.   By the 1760's,

tobacco purchasing had become a large-scale business, as

several Glasgow firms had established extensive chains of

stores.   The Cuninghame interests, one of the largest in

1774, operated seven stores in Maryland and fourteen in

Virginia, the latter located at Richmond, Amherst, and Rocky

---

52.   Robinson reported in April, 1773, that the price
of tobacco was 14 shillings per hundred pounds on the Rappahannock and Potomac, 16 shillings at Petersburg, and 18
shillings on the upper James.   James Robinson to William
Cuninghame & Company, April [?], 1773, Letterbook of William
Cuninghame & Company, II.

53.   Coulter, "Virginia Merchant," p. 105.

54.   Harry Piper reported in June of 1768 that "(if
many Ships does not come in) Tob[acc]o may probably rather

Ridge in the upper James valley, at Petersburg, Cabin Point, Mecklinburg Courthouse, Brunswick Courthouse, and Halifax on the south side of the James, at Dumfries on the Potomac, at Falmouth, Fredericksburg, Fauquier Courthouse, and Culpeper in the upper Rappahannock valley, and at Carolina Courthouse.[55] Companies controlled by John Glassford, another of the leading Glasgow "Tobacco Lords", operated stores throughout Maryland and Virginia, including those at Quantico, Dumfries, Fredericksburg, Falmouth, Colchester, Cabin Point, Rocky Ridge, Boyd's Hole, and Alexandria.[56]

The Scottish store system obviously required a considerable investment of capital. Eleven of the Cuninghame stores in Virginia were valued in 1775 at £11,450 sterling, not including goods, slaves, small craft, and wagons and horses. The Cuninghame firm also owned and operated at least six ocean-going ships for the Virginia trade alone.[57]

---

fall than rise ---". Piper to Dixon & Littledale, June 28, 1768, Letterbook of Harry Piper.

55. Price, "Glasgow in the Chesapeake Tobacco Trade," pp. 191-195.

56. [James Gourlay], A Glasgow Miscellany: The Tobacco Period in Glasgow, 1707-1775 (n.p., n.d.), pp. 28-29.

57. Price, "Glasgow in the Chesapeake Tobacco Trade," p. 194.

As an indication of the extensive business which these firms carried on, Table VIII shows the amounts of tobacco imported by each of forty-six Glasgow firms in 1774. The most important point, perhaps, is the concentration of a large portion of the trade in the hands of a relatively few firms. The six largest importers accounted for one-half of the total, the largest fifteen for over three-fourths. Data on exports from the Upper James naval district, 1773-1775, also reflect this pattern. Alexander Spiers & Company shipped more tobacco from this district than his two nearest rivals combined, while the three top exporters in 1773-1774 were responsible for as much tobacco as was sent to London and Liverpool together.[58]

Administration of a chain of stores required more organization than did maintenance of a connection with a single factor. In charge of the American operation was a chief factor - sometimes a partner, like Neil Jamieson, who supervised the Glassford stores in Virginia. Jamieson, in addition to his duties as chief factor, engaged in an extensive trade to the West Indies and southern Europe on

---

58. Thomson, "Tobacco Export of the Upper James," p. 397.

## TABLE VIII: LIST OF GLASGOW FIRMS AND IMPORTATIONS OF TOBACCO, 1774.

| Name of Firm | Hogsheads Imported |
|---|---|
| Alexander Spiers & Co. | 6,035 |
| John Glassford & Co. | 4,506 |
| Wm. Cuninghame & Co. | 3,881 |
| Dinwiddie, Crawford & Co. | 2,141 |
| John Hamilton & Co. | 1,967 |
| Oswald, Dennistoun & Co. | 1,701 |
| Henderson, McCaul & Co. | 1,587 |
| Colin Dunlop & Son | 1,455 |
| Cunninghame, Findlay & Co. | 1,290 |
| Bogle, Somervill & Co. | 1,270 |
| John Ballentine & Co. | 1,245 |
| James Donald & Co. | 1,264 |
| John McCall & Co. | 1,233 |
| Buchanan, Hastie & Co. | 1,085 |
| John Alston & Co. | 1,013 |
| James Ritchie & Co. | 903 |
| John McDowall & Co. | 790 |
| Scott, Donald & Co. | 657 |
| James Brown & Co. | 638 |
| Dreghorn, Murdoch & Co. | 502 |
| Jamieson, Johnston & Co. | 492 |
| Wm. Donald, Junr., & Co. | 485 |
| Dunlop, Crosse & Co. | 423 |
| Geo. and Andw. Buchanan & Co. | 403 |
| McCall, Dennistoun & Co. | 434 |
| Ramsay, Monteith & Co. | 392 |
| William Gray & Co. | 389 |
| James and Robert Buchanan | 364 |
| Thomson & Snodgrass | 329 |
| Thomas Dunlop & Co. | 300 |
| McCall, Smellie & Co. | 270 |
| Charles Reid | 190 |
| James Gammell & Co. | 137 |
| Alexander Donald & Co. | 109 |
| William Coats | 100 |

TABLE VIII (cont'd)

Andrew Sym & Co.------------------------------- 100
Andrew Brown---------------------------------- 99
Hugh Wylie & Co.------------------------------ 79
Cun, McKenzie & Co.--------------------------- 67
Baird, Weir & Co.----------------------------- 55

Simon Brown----------------------------------- 48
Baird, Hay & Co.------------------------------ 41
John Rowand & Co.----------------------------- 39
Hugh Wylie------------------------------------ 17
Andrew Hannah & Co.--------------------------- 10

James Baird, Senr.--------------------------- 8

Total imported-----------------------------40,543 Hhds.

Source:   [James Gourlay], A Glasgow Miscellany: The Tobacco
          Period in Glasgow, 1707-1775.  (n.p., n.d.), p. 26.

his own account.[59]

The chief factor was alert to locate new stores in likely places to attract customers. James Robinson, chief factor in Virginia for William Cuninghame and Company, indicated some of the strategy involved in store location in his instructions to the manager of a newly established store at Culpeper Courthouse:

> The more immediate motive for fixing this store
> was to be a Check on Mr Lawsons transactions at
> this store in the little fork of Rappahannock &
> to prevent any Other Company occupying a situ-
> ation at the Courthouse, which appears to your
> employers a suitable place for a Settlement
> being in a Good Tobacco County and in the Center
> of the county.[60]

The new storekeeper, though, was cautioned not to deal with people "who are Allready Customers to their [i.e., the Company's] Frederick[sbur]g or Falmouth Stores as they Can gain no additional Int[e]rest or influence by such." He was further instructed to build up his trade "with As little noise and parade as possible for fear of Alarming Others, and puting them on the same scheme before the store is well

---

    59.  Papers of Neil Jamieson (Library of Congress), passim.

    60.  James Robinson to William Cuninghame, October 8, 1771, Letterbook of William Cuninghame & Company, I.

established."61

A similar element of business strategy in store
location is shown in this communication from a Leedstown
factor to a London firm:

> There is now a Scotch Store fixed within about 6
> Miles of Leeds, the principal director has been
> pleased to give out that he has done it purely to
> take away the large Custom [of] your store at
> Leeds and to try if you have money to Carry on &
> support the Trade - This I think is a very [b]add
> declaration - I have it now in my power to fix a
> store at a good Wareho[use] on Poto[mac] about 6
> Miles above this Gentleman, w[hi]ch I am deter-
> mined to do.62

Each store in a chain was in charge of a salaried
manager. Probably representative were the arrangements
made by James Robinson in hiring storekeepers for the Cuninghame stores. For the management of the Culpeper store,
Robinson agreed to pay £60 sterling annually for a period
of five years.63 At Petersburg, where operations were more
extensive, an experienced storekeeper received £80 sterling
the first year, £90 the second year, and £100 annually for

---

61. Ibid.

62. Thomas Jett to Perkins, Buchanan & Brown, September
19, 1772, Letterbook of Thomas Jett, Jerdone Papers.

63. James Robinson to William Cuninghame & Company,
February 26, 1773, Letterbook of William Cuninghame & Company, II.

the remainder of the five year term.[64] In addition, the storekeeper was allowed living costs and an expense account. Alexander Blair expected to receive £20 "yearly for Incident Charges" in the operation of the Glassford store at Fredericks-burg.[65]

The storekeeper was expected to devote all of his time and energy to the operation of the store. Contracts usually provided that the storekeeper, as a salaried employee,

> be debarrd from all manner of Trade whatever di-
> rectly or indirectly on his own account or on
> any other account than his constitutents whose
> business of every kind he is to execute to the
> utmost of his ability as directed from time to
> time.[66]

James Robinson, in dismissing the manager of the Cuninghame store at Fauquier after the latter's marriage, maintained that the Company "cannot agree to be served by a married man, if a single one can be got, thinking the former must often be necessary call'd from their Business by his family

---

64. James Robinson to William Cuninghame & Company, September 24, 1773, *ibid.*, II.

65. Alexander Blair to Neil Jamieson, August 15, 1770, Papers of Neil Jamieson, XII, p. 2707.

66. James Robinson to Andrew Chalmer, May 31, 1771, Letterbook of William Cuninghame & Company, I.

affairs."[67]

The storekeeper was advised "Strongly from forming Acquaintance with the Idle and profligate part of your County." If business affairs did not keep the storekeeper busy, "any Intervall may be filled up much to his Improvement, by read[in]g Good Authors who Generally prove the best friends."[68] James Robinson promptly dismissed his storekeeper at Dumfries, who "gave a loose to dissipation" by "a purchase...of a Servant Girle which he kept for some time; and gaming to excess."[69]

In most cases, the post of storekeeper seems to have been filled by a young Scot. David Ross's sentiments probably reflected those of other merchants, who avoided hiring an American:

> from the manner of Educating the Youth of this Country, there [sic] untoward disposition & reluctance to confinement & drudgery induces me to intreat you not to Employ any more of them unless it be as a temporary assistant. I see from repeated experience that after a man has been at much pains with them & might reasonably expect

---

67. James Robinson to Bennett Price, September 11, 1768, ibid., I.

68. James Robinson to William Cuninghame, February 8, 1773, ibid., I.

69. James Robinson to John Turner, March 18, 1773, ibid., I.

> he had so moulded their dispositions as to act
> & think like himself, he is at once disappointed
> & finds after all he cannot deppend on them as
> their heads at that time a day are generally
> bent another way & they have too many passions
> to sacriffice before they can be serviceable
> to any man --- I speak in general terms -
> there are exceptions ---[70]

Some claimed that the large Scottish firms followed a policy

of nepotism, as indicated by this comment on locating a po-

sition in Virginia for a young man: "I was in hopes this

afternoon to have got him fix'd on York River in a very ex-

tensive & broad new Concern, but when the budget was open'd,

an advocate appeard for the Supra Cargoes brother, which

you may easily believe prevaild."[71]

Legend held that the road to wealth and success

in business began with employment as a storekeeper for a

tobacco firm, but James Parker, wealthy Norfolk merchant,

disagreed. In discussing a suitable position for the young

nephew of a friend in Scotland, Parker pointed out that un-

less the young man "had a Sufficienty to purchase a small

Share of one of those concerns after he had Served 4 or 5

Years in the business the Chance is against him" succeeding.

---

70. David Ross to John Hook, May 30, 1774, John Hook
Papers.

71. James Ingram to Charles Steuart, April 25, 1771,
Charles Steuart Papers, MS. 5026, p. 263.

Parker did not have fond memories of his own period of employment in the organization of Alexander Spiers, "the Mercantile God of Glasgow." "I was a factor, & had I been a
third or fourth Cuzin to Some of the principalls, I suppose,
with a patient, dilligent, Saving & Subservient disposition,
I might have jogged on in a State of dependance to this
day."[72]

In addition to the storekeeper, one or more clerks
or assistants were employed in the operation of the store.
Wages probably varied greatly according to experience.
Neil Jamieson engaged a clerk, evidently one with some experience, for his store at Boyd's Hole at an annual salary
of £40 sterling.[73] A beginning clerk might receive as
little as £5 per year, plus room and board, although annual
increases were provided in this case to bring the salary
to £25 in the final year of a five year contract.[74] Since
clerks were eligible for promotion within the organization,
managers of the Cuninghame stores were directed to transmit

---

72. James Parker to Charles Steuart, April 19, 1771,
ibid., MS.5040, p. 125.

73. Alex. Henderson to Neil Jamieson, December 26,
1774, Papers of Neil Jamieson, XX, p. 4660.

74. James Ingram to Charles Steuart, April 25, 1771,
Charles Steuart Papers, MS. 5026, p. 263.

annually to "the Company the Names of the Assistants under your directions; the time they have Served with their Characters & Capacitys in the most Impartial manner."[75] These data were then to be used as a basis for determining promotion of individuals to more responsible positions.

Negro slaves were used for work around the store. James Robinson employed fourteen slaves in the operation of the Cuninghame store at Falmouth: five as house servants, one to load and unload ships, one as carpenter, four to man a sloop, and three as crew of a schooner.[76]

Although the early stores were probably strictly utilitarian in architecture and furnishings, many of those of the 1770's were elaborate affairs. The Cuninghame store at Fredericksburg was valued in 1775 at £1,700, not including the goods in stock or slaves.[77] Arthur Morson estimated the value of the Falmouth property, consisting of

---

75. James Robinson to Francis Hay, October 13, 1772, Letterbook of William Cuninghame & Company, I.

76. James Robinson to William Cuninghame & Company, February 19, 1774, ibid., II.

77. Price, "Glasgow in the Chesapeake Tobacco Trade," p. 194. The Richmond store building which had belonged to the Cuninghame Company was large enough to be used in 1787 for meetings of the Senate and House of Delegates of Virginia.

a storehouse and more than one warehouse, which he used to conduct the business of the Glassford firm, at £440.[78] In 1774, Neil Jamieson considered leasing, as a site for the Glassford store, property at Cabin Point which included a dwelling, a two-story store building and counting house, kitchen, slave quarters, smoke house, stable and carriage house, pasture, and "a Large new Granarie," for an annual rent of £50 local currency.[79] When a company undertook trade in a new area, "Houses on Rent will answer better than to build for some time, untill it was known if the Trade turns out well."[80]

Operating costs of stores varied greatly, of course, but an account of costs of one of Neil Jamieson's stores in Pasquotank County, North Carolina, a produce rather than a tobacco area, does indicate something of the break-down of expenses. Of the total amount of £300 spent for store operation in 1772, the sum of £150 represented the

---

78. Arthur Morson to Glassford, Gordon, Monteath & Company, January 1, 1773, Papers of Neil Jamieson, XVI, p. 3731.

79. George Kerr to Neil Jamieson, March 2, 1774, Papers of Neil Jamieson, XIX, p. 4384.

80. James Robinson to John Turner, April 11, 1772, Letterbook of William Cuninghame & Company, I.

"Board Wages &c" of Matthias Ellegood "to Carry on the Management of a Store at his house," £20 "a Young Mans Board
&c," £10 for the hire of a slave, £40 for the purchase of
two horses, £40 for the use of storehouses and carts, and
£40 for "Victuales [and] Liquors in the House on the ocasion
through the year for Customers &c."[81]

The chief factor corresponded regularly with his
storekeepers, informing them of tobacco prices in Europe
and in other parts of the colony. In addition, he made
periodic personal visits to each of the stores and saw
many of the storekeepers at the Meetings of Merchants in
Williamsburg.

Each storekeeper was expected to keep the chief
factor and the principals in Britain regularly informed of
local developments. Adam Fleming, who operated the Glassford store at Cabin Point, wrote to Neil Jamieson:

> You think I dont writt you So frequently as I
> Should do, but I ashure you it is not through
> any neglect for at Present there is nothing to
> be purchased at all and my whole Study is to
> get the goods Disposed of to Good People which
> I Shall Indeavour to do as far as lys in my
> power.[82]

---

81. Matthias Ellegood to Neil Jamieson, June 7, 1773,
Papers of Neil Jamieson, XVIII, p. 4025.

82. Adam Fleming to Neil Jamieson, June 18, 1770,
ibid., XII, p. 2632.

Jamieson was probably a particularly demanding taskmaster.
Arthur Morson, his storekeeper at Falmouth, commented that
"in your next letter you will blame me for neglecting something or other & for the life of me I cannot recollect any-
thing further to add."[83]

Benjamin Franklin's philosophy that honesty is
the best policy was echoed in the prescriptions of the
Scottish traders. Robinson pointed out to a newly-appointed
Cuninghame storekeeper that to be "pointed and exact in
fulfilling your engagements or even your most trivial promises" would gain the "esteem, regard, & confidence" of customers, on which "alone a Large and extensive trade can be
acquired and Carried on."[84] Jamieson emphasized the importance of good customer relations to his young nephew,
who was loading a ship for Europe:

> I hope youl be careful to be as Obliging as in
> Power, to the Gentlemen in Shipping of the Cargo,
> dont by any means stand on triffeles to Carrie
> any dispute, ... To be obliging and good Naturd
> always gains friends & Esteem, but to act a Contra
> part, w[il]l. be hind[er]ing you[r] Self and us
> to[o], be not too prone to Pas[s]ion, weight a
> mat[t]er the[o]roughly before you venture to

---

83. Arthur Morson to Neil Jamieson, June 6, 1770, _ibid._,
XII, p. 2611.

84. James Robinson to John Turner, October 6, 1771,
Letterbook of William Cuninghame & Company, I.

> dispute, and even if you are right, do not glory
> too much in having the advantage, Young People
> are too fond of such things but as you are cau-
> tioned, I hope you['l]l be on your guard, and
> shun the Rack that many young men has Splitt
> upon.[85]

On the other hand, if the storekeeper held "too great an In-
timacy with any" of the customers, it "may be attended with
bad consequences." Visiting at planters' houses, James
Robinson felt, gave them "a pretence of takin[g] great
libertys at the Store."[86]

The storekeeper was responsible for carrying out
the policies formulated by the company in Britain and by
the chief factor in Virginia. Every storekeeper had to
act "pointedly to Orders, indeed if we do not there must
be an end of all Business, as they [i.e., the Cuninghame
firm in Glasgow] cannot be in any Settled State of Business
at home or know what to depend on, If we act at Random."[87]
The chief factor generally instructed the storekeeper in regard to tobacco price limits, which were based in turn upon
information sent to him from Britain as well as what he

---

85. Neil Jamieson & Company to Capt. Neil Jamieson,
April 6, 1767, Papers of Neil Jamieson, VIII, p. 1709.

86. James Robinson to William Cuninghame, October 8,
1771, Letterbook of William Cuninghame & Company, I.

87. James Robinson to "Dr. Sir," June 1, 1773, ibid., I.

learned at the Williamsburg Meetings.

The salaried manager as well as the independent storekeeper had many routine tasks to perform. James Robinson directed his storekeepers in this way:

> In the first of September Annually you are to take an exact Inventory of all the Goods & Effects under your Management, and to Shut the old & begin a new Sett of Books; transmitting to your Constituents as Early as may be in your power thereafter, and not latter than the first day of Feby following. Copy of said Inventory list of Outstanding debts due to & by the Store, Account Current founded thereon also Copy of your Cash Acctt, proffitt & Loss, or Intrest Acctt, and that of Charges of Merchandize, and any other paper, Book, or Account which may be required---[88]

In preparing their books, storekeepers were guided by the best accounting practices of the eighteenth century. "The saving of time or the reducing of clerical labor seems not to have been greatly considered," comments one authority.[89] The waste book recorded daily transactions as they occurred. These entries were then transferred to the journal, where they were expressed in terms of debit and credit, and then to the ledger. Here were collected the several items bearing on each account, placed so that the opposite parts of every

---

88.  James Robinson to Francis Hay, October 13, 1772, ibid., I.

89.  Voke, "Accounting Methods of Colonial Merchants in Virginia," p. 2.

account appeared on opposing sides of the folio. Since the
principal purpose of the storekeeper in maintaining records
was to keep track of debtors and creditors, the most important and most detailed ledger entries were accounts receivable and accounts payable. Profits and expenses were
determined from merchandize and commodity accounts. At
the completion of the accounting year, profits and expenses
were closed into a profit-and-loss account for determination
of a "net profit." It should be noted, though, that merchants, in arriving at this "net profit", did not usually
take into consideration overhead items such as depreciation
on property.[90]

The Purchase of Tobacco. Since the principal
purpose of the business operations of the stores was to
purchase tobacco, careful consideration had to be given to
the formulation of pricing policies on the basis of information about all the circumstances affecting supply and

---

90. Voke, "Accounting Methods of Colonial Merchants in
Virginia," pp. 6-8. Robert A. East, "The Business Entrepreneur in a Changing Colonial Economy, 1763-1795," Tasks
of Economic History, Supplemental Issue of The Journal of
Economic History, VI (1946), 24-25. See W. T. Baxter, The
House of Hancock: Business in Boston, 1724-1775 (Cambridge,
Mass.: Harvard University Press, 1945), pp. 35-38, for a
description of the accounting system used by the Hancocks
of Boston.

demand: the size and quality of the tobacco crop, the extent
of competition among traders in any given area, the amount
of shipping available, and the prices in Europe. At the
quarterly Meetings of Merchants, as we have seen, traders
and planters were able to assess all the data available on
market conditions on a colony-wide basis and to arrive at
a tentative market price.

The chief factor had the responsibility of co-
ordinating the purchases of all of the stores. Since a
primary consideration of the Scottish system was to have tobacco ready for prompt loading so as to keep turn-around
time of the ships at a minimum, James Robinson early in
the marketing season of 1772-1773 carefully prepared an estimate of the collections at all of the Cuninghame stores
in Virginia and then forwarded a proposed plan of shipping
to Glasgow. He calculated that over the year from September, 1772, to September, 1773, the stores in Rappahannock
region would purchase 1,970 hogsheads of tobacco, those on
the Potomac 1,300, and those on the James 1,980. He then
prepared a schedule for the Cuninghame ships to deliver
European goods to stores along each of the three rivers in
April and to load tobacco in December, April, June, and

September.[91] The estimate of collections and the proposed plan of shipping are set forth in Tables IX and X.

In his deal with the tobacco producer, the store-keeper might agree to pay in cash, in bills of exchange, in goods, or in some combination of these. Since money was scarce and a profit was made on the sale of goods, the purchaser tried to limit as much as possible his cash out-lay for tobacco. Generally, a higher price was given when the seller agreed to use the proceeds of the sale of his tobacco to purchase goods or to pay for goods previously bought on credit. Thus, one merchant found in 1773 that "at Richmond they give 18/- in discount of the Store debts & 16/- and 16/8 has been given Cash."[92] In other words, the planter who sold his tobacco for cash received 16 shillings or 16 shillings 8 pence per 100 pounds, while the man who used his tobacco to pay for goods in the store re-ceived 18 shillings in merchandise. Usually, some cash was necessary in order to attract sellers to the store. But

---

91. James Robinson to William Cuninghame & Company, October 18, 1772, Letterbook of William Cuninghame & Company, II.

92. David Ross to John Hook, July 8, 1773, Papers of John Hook. See also Coulter, "Virginia Merchant," pp. 106-108.

the proportion of cash involved in a deal varied with the specific position of the planter - those with top quality tobacco could sometimes exact all money - and with the competitive situation in the particular area. For example, in the depression of 1772-1773, William Cuninghame & Company limited sharply the proportion of cash used to purchase tobacco in their stores to one-fifth to one-quarter of the value of collections on the Rappahannock and Potomac, to one-quarter to one-third at Cabin Point and Petersburg, and to one-third to one-half in the Richmond area.[93]

Often cited is the charge of the planters that merchants customarily bought tobacco "at their own price," which they fixed at a "Shamefully low" rate.[94] Certainly, tobacco buyers made efforts to influence market prices through collusive action. For example, one Glasgow firm

---

93. James Robinson to John Nielson, August 19, 1772, Letterbook of William Cuninghame & Company, I.

94. N. F. Cabell, "Some Fragments of an Intended Report on the Post Revolutionary History of Agriculture in Virginia," with Notes by E. G. Swem, William and Mary Quarterly, 1st ser., XXVI (1918), 145-168. Cabell, writing in the nineteenth century, quotes "one of our elder and wiser brethren, ... one well versed in our history" as maintaining that "planters would thus soon come under bonds to those who were the sole purchasers of their produce; who bought it at their own price, and charged exorbitant profits for the goods and wares given in exchange." (p. 151)

TABLE IX:   ESTIMATE OF NUMBER OF HOGSHEADS OF TOBACCO TO
            BE COLLECTED AT THE VIRGINIA STORES OF WILLIAM
            CUNINGHAME & COMPANY, OCTOBER, 1772-OCTOBER,
            1773, MADE BY JAMES ROBINSON, CHIEF FACTOR.

|  | Total (Hhds) | Rappa- hannock | Potomac | James |
|---|---|---|---|---|
| Falmouth, Fauquier, Culpeper | 1,420 | 870 | 550 | |
| Fredericksburg | 1,100 | 1,100 | | |
| Dumfries | 750 | | 750 | |
| Cabin Point, Brunswick, Granville | 550 | | | 550 |
| Petersburg, Halifax, Mecklinburgh | 880 | | | 880 |
| Rocky Ridge | 900 | | | 900 |
| Richmond | 350 | | | 350 |
| | 5,250 | 1,970 | 1,300 | 1,980 |

Source:   James Robinson to William Cuninghame & Company,
          October 18, 1772, Letterbook of William Cuninghame
          & Company, II.

TABLE X:  PROPOSED PLAN OF SHIPPING TOBACCO OF WILLIAM
CUNINGHAME & COMPANY, OCTOBER, 1772-OCTOBER, 1773,
MADE BY JAMES ROBINSON, CHIEF FACTOR

[HOGSHEADS]

|  | Arrive | Rappa-hannock | Potomac | James |
|---|---|---|---|---|
| Cochrane via Havre de Grace | Dec. | | | 460 |
| Janett via France | Dec. | | 390 | |
| Cuninghame straight out | Dec. | 500 | | |
| Neptune [with] goods | April | | | 460 |
| Venus [with] goods | April | | 450 | |
| Ocean [with] goods [from] London | April | 560 | | |
| Cochrane | June | 460 | | |
| Cuninghame | June | | | 500 |
| Neptune | Sept. | | 460 | |
| Venus | Sept. | 450 | | |
| Ocean | Sept. | | | 560 |
|  |  | 1,970 | 1,300 | 1,980 |

Source:  James Robinson to William Cuninghame & Company,
October 18, 1772, Letterbook of William Cuninghame
& Company, II.

urged factors in Virginia to "meet and consult together and jointly pursue the most effectual measures for reducing the price of Tobacco." The missive went on to point out that until prices in the colony were lowered, the quantity produced would not be lessened; "and until the quantity be lessened, the price will not rise at home." The Scottish merchants were convinced that in the long run "the lessening [of] the quantity will...prove [to] the Advantage of the Planters" as well as to the interest of the traders.[95] Granted that the tobacco traders "would be monopolists if they could,"[96] how did they attempt to lessen competition and how effective were their efforts to manipulate the market to their own advantage?

Merchants sometimes formed "gentlemen's agreements" for the purpose of holding the price of tobacco to a definite limit. To cite one example, the buyers at Dumfries proposed in May, 1769, that 22/6 per 100 pounds be paid for tobacco until July 1, at which date the price was to drop

---

95. John McCall & James Ritchie & Company to William Snodgrass, Robinson Daingerfield, Andrew Crawford, and James Anderson, February 15, 1765, Caroline County Appeals and Land Cases, 1787-1807 (Virginia State Library Archives).

96. Josiah Tucker, The Elements of Commerce (1755), quoted in Vernon A. Mund, Monopoly: A History and Theory (Princeton: Princeton University Press, 1933), p. 42. Tucker believed that businessmen strove for monopoly to escape competition.

to 20/-. Merchants at Falmouth agreed to the limits suggested,
but argued that the price should be lowered after June 10,
since planters on the Rappahannock brought their tobacco
to market earlier than those on the Potomac. Therefore,
Falmouth purchasers would derive "little or no advantage
from the measure for if we give 22/6 to the first of July,
we may as well continue it to the close" of the marketing
season. Furthermore, lowering the price at the earlier
date would "establish a precedent which may be attended
with Good Consequences hereafter," since planters would be
discouraged from holding their tobacco back in hopes of a
better price. The agreement was to include merchants not
only in Falmouth and Dumfries, but also those in Fredericksburg and in the smaller centers of Boyd's Hole and Fauquier
Courthouse. Robinson felt that the price drop after June
10 might appear to the planter to "be rather too abrupt,"
but he hoped that the good prospects for the next crop, al-
ready well on the way, would convince the producer that the
price of 20 shillings per 100 pounds was "more than adequate to the value of Tobacco." The Cuninghame chief
factor concluded a letter to one of his storekeepers with
the hope that "no man will give more than what may be mu-
tually agreed upon either in the price now or that which is

to be fixed hereafter."[97]

However, the success of such attempts to avoid
the burdens of competition was subject to several limita-
tions. Undoubtedly, agreements to limit prices were observed fairly well when the crop was large and the price in
European markets depressed. When demand was brisk, though,
efforts at price fixing were not likely to be attended with
success for the buyers. As Robinson pointed out in 1772,
"so great is the demand for Tobacco all over the colony
arising from the Number of Ships imployed in the Trade,
that the Planter has been able to establish his own terms."[98]
If merchants could conclude agreements on the price to be
paid for tobacco, producers might also form an association
to fix selling prices when economic conditions were favor-
able to them, as planters along the Potomac attempted to do
in 1770.[99] In the same way that buyers cited lower prices
paid by French and other European buyers as justification

---

97. James Robinson to J. Nielson, May 25, 1769, Letterbook of William Cuninghame & Company, I.

98. James Robinson to Cuninghame & Company, June 1,
1772, Letterbook of William Cuninghame & Company, II.

99. David J. Mays, Edmund Pendleton, 1721-1803: A Biography (Cambridge, Mass.: Harvard University Press, 1952),
I, 116.

for reductions in prices paid to producers, planters tried to take advantage of reports about poor crop prospects to hold out for higher prices. After bad weather conditions in the fall of 1769, Robinson wrote that "the planter and seller in the Country we may believe will make what they Can of the Circumstances of the Storm in order to enhance the Value of their Commoditys and they may possibly succeed for some time."[100]

At times, merchants in neighboring communities had difficulty in agreeing upon a price which they would pay for tobacco. For example, the Falmouth buyers set a rate of 18 shillings per 100 pounds in the spring of 1772, but the effort at price-fixing failed when the purchasers in nearby Fredericksburg refused to ratify this decision. Even when Fredericksburg and Falmouth merchants eventually agreed on the 18 shilling price, planters could sell at Port Royal, twenty miles distant, for 20 shillings.[101]

In spite of the concentration of a large share of the tobacco trade in the hands of a few firms, as indicated

---

100. James Robinson to William Henderson, October 10, 1769, Letterbook of William Cuninghame & Company, I.

101. James Robinson to Cuninghame & Company, June 1, 1772, ibid., II. Mays, Pendleton, I, 116.

above, the number of purchasers was in many instances too great to permit monopolistic practices to succeed. An Alexandria buyer lamented in 1770 that "the misfortune of this Trade is, we are too much subjected to the caprice of a few, because there are too many purchasers pushing one another." Three years later, he maintained that he had never bid up the market price, but that he "must follow if I purchase, & am sorry to observe that a few wrong headed Men have it in their power to effect the price."[102]

Newly established merchants often offered a price above the prevailing market rate in order to get established. William Allason followed this practice when he entered business in Falmouth in 1760, although he denounced it when it was used by others in later years.[103] Robinson summed up the impact of new stores on the competitive situation in the Fredericksburg-Falmouth area in 1769 in this way:

> I am afraid the price given for these Collections will be extravagently high from the new Stores fix'd here and Fredericks[bur]g at which last place since you was there Mr. James Robb has opend Stores. It is Rumor'd that Mr Briggs Offered 25/ p Cwt to the

---

102. Harry Piper to Dixon & Littledale, April 3, 1770 and June 1, 1772, Letterbook of Harry Piper.

103. Edith E. B. Thomson, "A Scottish Merchant in Falmouth in the Eighteenth Century," Virginia Magazine of History and Biography, XXXIX (1931), 117.

> planter and 6 d p Cwt more than any person
> here will give. If this is the truth judge
> what will be our Condition.[104]

In early 1770, the Cuninghame manager maintained that "altho'
we refuse to take Tobacco at present from the Planters at
25/- yet should our new Stores Continue to give that price,
so must we also."[105]

Furthermore, companies which operated several
stores saw that competitive advantages could be derived
from local price-fixing agreements. Robinson pointed out
that the price reduction effected by Dumfries buyers in the
summer of 1770 was "a favourable Circumstance" for increasing
the business of the recently-established Cuninghame store
at Fauquier Courthouse, since planters in that county would
now find it less desirable to do business at Dumfries.[106]

Still another factor of importance to the ability
of merchants to hold prices in line was the amount of shipping available. As Piper pointed out, "if many Ships does

---

104. James Robinson to William Henderson, October 10,
1769, Letterbook of William Cuninghame & Company, I.

105. James Robinson to William Henderson, February 12,
1770, ibid.

106. James Robinson to John Turner, July 12, 1770,
ibid.

not come in, Tobacco may probably rather fall than rise."[107]
Robinson indicated the abundant shipping available as the
major cause of difficulty to the Cuninghame store at Dumfries.
The storekeeper there was thus "obliged to push for Tobacco:
and to take it from his Customers on unfavourable terms;
which will unavoidably be the Consequence to Any Store by
being Encumbered with a Quick Succession of Shipping."[108]
Holding the company's ship until the next season was a
costly alternative to purchasing tobacco, even at an un-
attractive price.

Finally, many planters were able to consign their
tobacco to British merchants if they felt that prices in
Virginia were unfavorable, as they did in northern Virginia
in 1773. Piper reported that "many of our Planters are
Shipping to London, as they can't think of taking the Price
in the Country." However, Piper maintained that the London
merchants, "who are Chartering all the Vessels they can
meet with, at a pretty high freight," were not concerned
about the lowered price which consigning planters might

---

107. Harry Piper to Dixon & Littledale, June 28, 1768,
Letterbook of Harry Piper.

108. James Robinson to Francis Hay, October 13, 1772,
Letterbook of William Cuninghame & Company, I.

receive as a result of the large amount of tobacco arriving at market.[109]

From a business point of view, the tobacco buyer had not only a short-run interest in purchasing as much tobacco at as low a price as possible but also a long-run interest in establishing and maintaining a market for his goods and services. Shrewd entrepreneurs engaged in a competitive business, as were these traders, recognized that profits derived from efficient use of the capital invested in ships, stores, and goods. Robinson, writing to a new storekeeper in 1769, summarized the Cuninghame policy, and what was likely the policy of other tobacco purchasers, in this way: "Such is the Course of our Trade that we must Endeavour to buy all the Tobacco we Can at the different Stores at what Ever is the marcatt price, the Company not being willing to lose any of their Interest in this Branch to any Person what ever."[110]

---

109. Harry Piper to Dixon & Littledale, July 1 and July 17, 1773, Letterbook of Harry Piper.

110. James Robinson to John Turner, April 22, 1769, Letterbook of William Cuninghame & Company, I.

## B.  THE PRODUCE TRADE

Though tobacco production provided the base of
the Virginia economy throughout the colonial period, other
commodities, particularly foodstuffs, assumed importance
among Virginia's exports after 1750.  Indeed, Virginians
had long searched for other staples to relieve their depend-
ence on a one-crop economy.  To some extent, the growth in
the production of foodstuffs was because of soil exhaustion
and dissatisfaction with tobacco prices in the Tidewater.
But, as Gray points out, the expansion of wheat-growing resulted mainly from the settlement of the Piedmont.[111]  By
the 1770's Roger Atkinson was writing enthusiastically to
an English correspondent: "It is w[i]th great pleasure I
acq[uain]t you, that We have now got another Staple...viz
Wheat, w[hi]ch will I believe in a little time be equal,
if not superior to Tob[acc]o...We shall in a few years make
more [wheat] in Virginia, than all the Province of Pennsylvania put together."[112]

---

111. Gray, Agriculture in the Southern United States to
1860, I, 166-169.  See also, Craven, Soil Exhaustion, pp. 65-68.

112.  Roger Atkinson to Lyonel & Samuel Hyde, August 25,
1772, Letterbook of Roger Atkinson.  James Robinson in 1774
urged the Cuninghame tobacco firm of Glasgow to purchase
wheat on a large scale; a few years earlier, he had maintained that the store system existed primarily to purchase

In addition, Virginia by the 1760's and 1770's was exporting considerable amounts of corn, meat, peas, beans, lard, and butter. Exports other than foodstuffs, especially lumber products in the form of staves, shingles, and pine boards were also important. Neil Jamieson noted that "not one ship ever Loaded in Virginia but had some lumber on board...to dunnage with."[113] Tar and turpentine, skins, and iron also figured in the colony's exports, although most of these items, except iron, were the products of North Carolina.

Hopes had been held at various times in the eighteenth century that other products would become important export staples, but these hopes were not realized. A Falmouth storekeeper maintained in 1764, on receiving news of the granting by the British government of a bounty for hemp, that the "Commodity will in a few years be a Staple up this way."[114] Virginia did become the leading hemp producer in North America, but most of the 5,000 tons produced annually

---

tobacco. James Robinson to William Cuninghame & Company, April 29, 1774, Letterbook of William Cuninghame & Company, II.

113. Neil Jamieson to Robert Alexander, May 11, 1781, Chalmers Collection (New York Public Library). Dunnage is material used to prevent damage to the cargo.

114. Arthur Morson to Neil Jamieson, December 6, 1764, Papers of Neil Jamieson, IV, p. 891.

in the years just prior to the American Revolution were processed and consumed in the colony.[115] Indigo had been reported in the 1750's to be sure of becoming an important export of the colony, again because of the belief that a British bounty would stimulate its production, but Virginians became dissatisfied with the low prices which the product received in English markets and largely abandoned its production after 1765.[116]

While the tobacco trade was controlled by British merchants and handled in British ships, the produce trade was carried on by American merchants, those resident in Virginia as well as in other colonies. Also, many of the factors who worked for British tobacco houses purchased and sold foodstuffs and other commodities on their own account.[117]

Major Markets. Great Britain was the destination of most of the pig iron, tar, and skins, as well as a sizeable

---

115. G. Melvin Herndon, "Hemp in Colonial Virginia," Agricultural History, XXXVII (1963), 86-93.

116. Charles Steuart to Benjamin Walker, September 29, 1756, Letterbook of Charles Steuart. Middleton, Tobacco Coast, p. 175.

117. Coulter, "Virginia Merchant," pp. 55-57. Middleton, Tobacco Coast, pp. 198-202.

amount of the staves, exported from Virginia. But Britain
imported colonial foodstuffs only when shortages existed in
the domestic market. The Corn Laws provided for low duties
to permit the importation of American grain only when the
price rose above a certain level.[118] Thus, only twenty-
four bushels of wheat were exported from Virginia to Great
Britain in 1772, but over 55,000 bushels were shipped in
1768 and nearly 34,000 in 1771.[119]

Virginia exporters had to search for other markets
than Britain for foodstuffs, notably the West Indies and
southern Europe. The islands in the Caribbean accounted
in 1772 for over one-half of Virginia's shipments of corn,
nearly one-third of the lard, most of the shingles and pine
planks and boards, over one-half of the staves, nearly two-
thirds of the turpentine, and over three-fourths of the
meat and peas. Most of the West Indian trade of Virginia,
like that of the other mainland colonies, was carried on by
ships which shuttled back and forth between the mainland

---

118. E. Lipson, The Economic History of England (London:
Adam & Charles Black, 1948), II, 461-464.

119. See Appendix A. Unless otherwise indicated, references to Virginia exports in 1772 are based upon these
data. The figures include the re-export of some products
of North Carolina origin. The data for 1768 and 1771 are
from Thomson, "Merchant in Virginia," p. 252.

and the Islands.[120] As Charles Steuart noted in a letter to a West Indian correspondent in 1752, a "Vessell continually imployed in the trade from hence to your Island with full freights each way, may under good management clear money."[121] Each cargo was varied as to the types of commodities included, as indicated by the following invoice of a shipment made by Neil Jamieson from Norfolk to St. Christopher in 1766:

| Commodity | Quantity | Value |
|---|---|---|
| Indian Corn | 1,040 bushels | £166. 8. |
| Pickled Pork | 50 barrels | 146. 5. |
| Flour | 23,936 pounds (100 barrels) | 179.10. 4 |
| Casks for Flour | 100 | 8. 6. 8 |
| Bread | 13,955 pounds (100 barrels) | 104.13. 2 |
| Barrels for Bread | 100 | 10. |
| Red Oak Hogshead Staves | 8,400 (shipped as 7,000) | 19. 5. |

---

120. This discussion of the West Indian trade of Virginia is based largely upon the correspondence of Neil Jamieson, particularly from 1765 to 1770. For a general picture of the trade between the West Indies and the North American mainland, see Richard Pares, Yankees and Creoles: The Trade Between North America and the West Indies before the American Revolution (Cambridge: Harvard University Press, 1956) and James B. Hedges, The Browns of Providence Plantations: Colonial Years (Cambridge: Harvard University Press, 1952), Chapter 2.

121. Charles Steuart to Andrew Armour, February 14, 1752, Letterbook of Charles Steuart, I.

| Commodity | Quantity | Value |
|-----------|----------|-------|
| Shingles | 31,500 | 22. -. 1 |

TOTAL                                                    656. 8. 5
Commission at 5%                          32.16. 5
689. 4.10. [122]

In the West Indian trade, the Virginia merchant might be the owner of the cargo, assuming the costs and risks of transporting the commodities to their ultimate market, or he might act as an agent for a West Indian firm. This latter was the case in the shipment cited above, in which the cargo had been assembled by Jamieson, who received a commission of 5 per cent of the value of the commodities. Very likely, the St. Christopher merchants had sent a cargo of West Indian goods to be sold by Jamieson, again for a commission, and had ordered the proceeds of the sale to be invested in Virginia commodities. Where the Virginia merchant acted as a principal, he consigned a cargo to a West Indian firm, which sold the commodities for a commission. [123]

---

122. Invoice of Sundries Shipped by Neil Jamieson & Compy on Board the Schooner Potby Capt Anderson by order and for Account and Risque of Messrs. Henderson & Phillips Mercht. in St. Christophers, June 9, 1766, Papers of Neil Jamieson, VII, p. 1461.

123. See Stuart Bruchey, "Success and Failure Factors: American Merchants in Foreign Trade in the Eighteenth and Early Nineteenth Centuries," Business History Review, XXXII (1958), 272-292, for a discussion of the important role of the resident agent in foreign trade.

The ship captain, though, might be given orders to proceed to another island if the first market proved unfavorable. Returns were made in West Indian produce, purchased by the resident agent in the island (or perhaps by the ship captain), in bills of exchange on Britain, or in specie, depending upon the market situation at the time of the shipment.

Southern Europe and the "Wine Islands" (Madeira and the Canaries) also constituted important markets for Virginia products. In 1772, exports to this area accounted for nearly one-half of the total of wheat, over one-third of bread and flour, and smaller amounts of corn and lumber.

But trade with southern Europe was marked by sharp fluctuations, the volume depending upon the size of local crops and the amount of imports from normal suppliers in Italy, Turkey, and north Africa. Thus wheat shipments from Virginia to southern Europe totalled 65,763 bushels in 1768, 335,945 in 1769, 174,045 in 1770, and 133,743 in 1771.[124]

Correspondents discussed at great length the European conditions which determined prospects for profitable exportations of American foodstuffs to this area. Mayne & Company wrote from Lisbon in the summer of 1769:

---

124. Thomson, "Merchant in Virginia," p. 252.

"Daily advices from the Country confirm the shortness of our Crops so that there must be a demand for foreign grain."[125] Similarly, the demand for American grain was expected to increase at this time in Barcelona, as "no supplys can be expected from the Levant on account of the Turks being in warr with the Russians."[126] A Cadiz businessman commented in 1770 that the harvest "of the Crops in Italy Sicily & the West of France & England may have some Influence upon the Span: & Portugal marketts."[127] On the other hand, it was reported from Lisbon in 1772 that "our imports of wheat from your side have been very inconsiderable by being pretty well supplied with Sicily, Northern & some Country Wheat of the late crop."[128]

These fluctuations had also characterized Virginia's trade with southern Europe and Madeira in earlier decades. For example, Charles Steuart wrote in 1752 that

---

125. Mayne & Company to Neil Jamieson, July 25, 1769, Papers of Neil Jamieson, X, p. 2270.

126. March & Tilebein to Neil Jamieson, July 5, 1769, ibid., X, p. 2261.

127. Tesson Welsh & Company to Neil Jamieson, June 26, 1770, ibid., XII, p. 2591.

128. Mayne & Company to Neil Jamieson, October 10, 1772, ibid., XVI, p. 3595.

the "Demand for Grain in Madeira and Europe has diverted the Trade a good deal from the west India Islands this winter." But eight years later, he reported that "indiff[eren]t prospects for our product in Mad[eir]a has lessened and allmost entirely broke off our trade thither."[129]

Not only did prospects for profitable trade with southern Europe fluctuate from year to year, but they altered abruptly during a season as demand was met by shipments. Even in the large Lisbon market, caution was in order when a particular commodity was in great demand, as flour was in the summer of 1769. Thus, Mayne & Company wrote to Jamieson:

> A Glut of that Commodity will follow of course
> in that case [i.e., of speculative shipments
> made because of news of the shortage], where-
> fore we would you be cautious of sending us
> whole Cargos of Flour notwithstanding the en-
> couragement we gave you lately to do so, but
> content yourselves with putting a few hundred
> Bar[rel]s of it between decks of such Ships as
> you may send us with Wheat in proportion to the
> size of the Vessels.[130]

One way to reduce the risk of hitting a market

---

129. Charles Steuart to [Mrs. Ninvielle and Company], January 9, 1752; to Robert Scott, February 22, 1760, Letterbooks of Charles Steuart, I, II.

130. Mayne & Company to Neil Jamieson, August 19, 1769, Papers of Neil Jamieson, X, p. 2291.

glutted by excessive shipments of a particular commodity
was to send an assorted cargo. Jamieson's correspondent
in Madeira pointed out in 1764 that "Our limited market
permits not of our trusting to any one Commodity, tho sometimes it might hit...but it is a chance if we are not gluted
as soon as it begins to come in." Thus, he recommended the
following assortment of cargo: wheat, 1,000 bushels; Indian
corn, 1,000 bushels; flour, 100 barrels; beeswax, 6-8 barrels; pork, 40-50 barrels; rice, 30-50 hogsheads; white oak
pipe staves, 3-4,000; hogshead and barrel staves, 3-4,000;
and pine boards, 2,000 feet.[131]

As in the West Indian trade, the cargo was consigned to a European firm, which sold the commodities on
commission. Sometimes, though, the foreign houses requested
a one-quarter to one-half interest in cargoes shipped by
Virginia firms, provided the commodities be purchased within specified price limits. For example, Mayne & Company
directed Jamieson in 1769 in this way:

> You apprehend rightly that when any of your Neigh-
> bours are loading Wheat or Flour for this Market,
> we would have you Interest us as farr as One
> fourth or One Third wherein, tho you should have

---

131.  Fergusson, Murdock & Company to Neil Jamieson,
April 8, 1764, ibid., IV, pp. 701-702.

no Share yourself, provided the Commodities be of
a good quality, & come within our limits; that
the Vessel is sufficient & the whole Cargo be ad-
dressed to us.[132]

Returns were made in southern European products, particularly

wine and salt, in bills of exchange on London, in cash, or

in a combination of these.

Much trust had to be placed in the foreign agent's

integrity and business ability. Thus, personal contact and

recommendation were important in arranging business relation-

ships. When Jamieson first became interested in the trade

with southern Europe, he made inquiry of his regular London

correspondent as to reliable houses.[133] Before he started

to trade with Italy, Jamieson called personally upon John

Henry Noble of London, whose firm had a branch in Leghorn

(Otto Franck & Company.) Noble also referred Jamieson to

John & Francis Baring & Company, his bankers, for recommen-

dations as to the firm's financial standing and ability to

make prompt remittances.[134] Generally, Norfolk merchants,

---

132. Mayne & Company to Neil Jamieson, September 28,
1769, ibid., XI, pp. 2333-2336.

133. Robert & Robert Bogle & Scott to Neil Jamieson,
October 24, 1764, ibid., IV, pp. 861-862.

134. John Henry Noble to Neil Jamieson, September 3,
1772, ibid., XVI, p. 3560. John Henry Noble to John Glassford & Company, November 9, 1772, ibid., XVI, pp. 3632-3633.

like those of other American ports dealt with British firms or branches of British houses located in southern Europe.[135]

Virginia also exported its commodities to other colonies on the North American mainland. The "Coastways" trade in 1772 accounted for over one-half of the Old Dominion's wheat shipments, about one-third of the corn, one-fifth of the meat, most of the butter and lard, and small amounts of lumber, tar, and turpentine. In most cases, these products were probably used by the business-men of other colonies in their trade with the West Indies and southern Europe.[136]

The merchants of Philadelphia, the major grain and flour market on the continent, played a particularly important role in the wheat trade of Virginia. Thus, the Virginia merchants ordered the publication in the Pennsylvania Gazette of their resolution of November, 1772,

---

135. Jamieson consigned cargoes to Mayne & Company of Lisbon, March & Tilebein in Barcelona, Tesson Welsh in Cadiz, Fergusson, Murdock & Company in Madeira, and Otto Franck & Company in Leghorn. For an illustration of the kinds of problems that arose when American merchants attempted to deal with foreigners, see James H. Soltow, "Thomas Riche's 'Adventure' in French Guiana, 1764-1766," Pennsylvania Magazine of History and Biography, LXXXIII (1959), 409-419.

136. Middleton, Tobacco Coast, p. 199.

prescribing the days of the Williamsburg Meetings.[137]  The

comments of businessmen also testify to the significance of

the activity of the Philadelphians.  For example, Robert

Pleasants of Curles attributed the brisk demand for Vir-

ginia wheat in 1773 "chiefly to fulfill Orders from

Phila[delphia]."[138]  James Robinson reported that one

Philadelphia firm purchased 100,000 bushels of wheat, and

another 30,000, during the fall and winter of 1773-1774.[139]

　　　　Philadelphia merchants normally placed orders

with their counterparts in Virginia.  In 1763, Stewart

Duncan & Company of Philadelphia, inquiring of Neil Jamieson

the price of Virginia wheat, indicated that "sh[oul]d Your

Terms Suit us we may probably Contract w[it]h You for a

Considerable Quantity to be delivered at Sundry Times."[140]

A decade later, Robinson reported that Inglis & Long of

Norfolk were purchasing large quantities of wheat for Willing

---

137.　Virginia Gazette (Purdie & Dixon), November 26,
1772.

138.　Robert Pleasants to "Brother," December 7, 1773,
Letterbook of Robert Pleasants.

139.　James Robinson to William Cuninghame & Company,
February 7, 1774, Letterbook of William Cuninghame & Company,
II.

140.　Stewart Duncan & Company to Neil Jamieson, October
3, 1765, Papers of Neil Jamieson, V, p. 1186.

& Morris of Philadelphia.[141] But sometimes Virginians consigned wheat to the Philadelphia market, as did Robert
Pleasants in 1772 with "a view of Employing our new Vessel,
and in hope of geting the prices lately going for wheat in
Phila[delphia]."[142]

Pennsylvanians usually shipped a large portion of
their wheat purchases directly to foreign markets. But the
high price of wheat on the Philadelphia market in 1772,
when it reached a peak for the colonial period, probably
made it profitable to ship the commodity to that northern
city.[143] Thus, the figure for the "coastways" export of
wheat in 1772 may have been abnormally high.

---

141. James Robinson to William Cuninghame & Company,
February 7, 1774, Letterbook of William Cuninghame & Company, II.

142. Robert Pleasants to "Brother," August 3, 1772,
"Letters of Robert Pleasants," William and Mary Quarterly,
2d ser., II, 268; and Robert Pleasants to James Pemberton,
October 8, 1773, Letterbook of Robert Pleasants.

143. Arthur L. Jensen, The Maritime Commerce of Colonial Philadelphia (Madison: The State Historical Society
of Wisconsin, 1963), pp. 77-78. Anne Bezanson, Robert D.
Gray, and Miriam Hussey, Prices in Colonial Pennsylvania
(Philadelphia: University of Pennsylvania Press, 1935), p. 46.
According to Jensen, "only very low prices in Virginia or
Maryland and very high prices in Philadelphia made it profitable to send wheat coastwise to Philadelphia. Upon occasion there was sufficient differential in price in the two
areas to encourage such shipments, but such conditions were
distinctly abnormal."

Other mainland colonies probably accounted for a considerably smaller share of Virginia's trade. But in the 1760's and 1770's Benjamin Harrison of Charles City County and William Holt of James City County made shipments of wheat, corn, and flour to William Palfrey of Boston. Holt, who operated a flour mill near Williamsburg, proposed in 1765 to keep a "Vessel constantly Running backward, & forward" between his mill and Boston.[144] Also, there was a regular but relatively small flow of trade to New York.[145]

Purchasing of Produce. Although a number of Virginia ports participated in the export of wheat, corn, meat, and other agricultural commodities, Norfolk had established predominance in the trade by the 1760's. Governor Fauquier maintained in 1764 that Norfolk had engrossed the grain trade of the colony.[146]

Neil Jamieson pointed out that on the eve of the

---

144. William Holt to William Palfrey, March 2, 1765, Palfrey Papers (Harvard University Library).

145. Virginia D. Harrington, The New York Merchant on the Eve of the American Revolution (New York: Columbia University Press, 1935), pp. 208-209.

146. Governor Fauquier to Board of Trade, January 30, 1764, quoted in Thomas J. Wertenbaker, Norfolk: Historic Southern Port (Durham: Duke University Press, 1931), p. 38n.

American Revolution "the greatest proportion of the wheat
and Corn as well as some of the Tobacco and Naval Stores"
were loaded at Norfolk and that "this trade greatly Increas'd"
in the years just before the war. He explained that "the
Expence of Country freight was lower to Norfolk than from
one River to another, so that by loading at Norfolk when
the Cargo laid in different Rivers, was cheaper and Sooner
performed than if the ship lay in any other part of the
Country."[147]

For the storage of produce, Norfolk merchants
built an extensive system of wharves and warehouses. The
wharf of William Orange, for example, was said to be "one
of the greatest works of the kind that ever had been erected
in that Country." It contained eleven storehouses and was
valued in 1774 at £5,000 - 6,000.[148] Such facilities provided a real convenience for, unlike the tobacco trade,
there were no public warehouses on the rivers for storage
of produce until export.

The correspondence of Neil Jamieson, Norfolk

---

147. Neil Jamieson to Robert Alexander, May 11, 1781,
Chalmers Collection.

148. Memorial of William Orange, American Loyalist Transcripts (New York Public Library), LVIII, pp. 270-295.

merchant, illustrates well the methods of collecting country produce. Jamieson used the Glassford stores, which he supervised for the Scottish tobacco firm, to organize and conduct an extensive business in wheat, flour, corn, and other produce. Adam Fleming at Cabin Point, Arthur Morson at Falmouth, and Alexander Cuninghame at Fredericksburg made regular shipments of these commodities to Norfolk. Much of the produce represented payment for goods which the storekeeper sold to planters and farmers in the neighborhood. The following communication is representative of the periodic reports made by Fleming:

> It is Realy impossible for me to Say what Quantity of Corn Pease &c I may Receive this Winter as the Most of these Comoditys that I Collect is purchased intirly with West India Commoditys & Salt (perticularly Brown Sugar & Molasses)[149]

From time to time, Fleming was ordered to make specific purchases from producers or neighboring storekeepers, as in this case:

> I Observe you will want 6000 Bushels Indian Corn nixt Month, I Coud have purchased a great deal of Corn before this time, but they have got a Notion that Corn will bring more then 10/ p Barrel in a Short time therefore the most of them will not

---

149. Adam Fleming to James Glassford, September 6, 1772, Papers of Neil Jamieson, XVI, p. 3562.

Sell there Corn at present under 12/6[150]

Jamieson also dealt extensively with independent storekeepers throughout Virginia, Maryland, and North Carolina.  He received frequent letters offering commodities for sale, as in the following inquiry from a Fredericksburg merchant:

> I have got 200 Barrels Indian Corn for Sale...if you are in want you may have it...let me know the very utmost you'll give as we are at a distance and cannot chassen much About it.[151]

In one case, Jamieson was offered all or a considerable part of the annual output of a merchant flour mill, located near Petersburg, which milled 10,000 bushels of wheat per year.[152]  More often, Jamieson sent orders to correspondents when he was in need of a specific amount of produce.  A Petersburg storekeeper wrote to him in 1765:  "Your last came too late to make a purchase of Flour on your terms....  Theres no possibility of making a Purchase of the Q[uantit]y

---

150.  Adam Fleming to Neil Jamieson, January 15, 1771, ibid., XIII, p. 2875.

151.  James Somervell to Neil Jamieson, February 24, 1767, ibid., VIII, p. 1890.

152.  Thomas Irving to Neil Jamieson, October 16, 1774, ibid., XX, p. 4614.

of Pork you mention."[153]

Jamieson evidently used the produce derived from the regular trade at the Glassford stores as a nucleus of his stock of export commodities and purchased from other suppliers when a particular commodity was needed. This policy is well illustrated by the following letter from an Alexandria merchant:

> I only Recd. yours of the 26th. Novr. yisterday and had [smudged] ten days ago I could have Sent you near two hund. barrels of verie Good flower which I sold here at 13/10 pr. Cwt. when I was at your place I had no incuragement to depend on any market with you but had you desired me to have purchased flower on your accot. I could have had by this time about 200 Ct or perhaps more at the Reate of 12/6 for Ready Money which is the Lowest price here...if in case you will want any flower in the spring and that your price will be agreable or worth while I can perhaps purchase some by that time but to purchase at an uncertainty I will not do but will be glade if you would as soon as posible advise me of the price of that article with you at all times.[154]

Exporting farm produce presented problems not encountered in the tobacco trade. One of the most important involved storage, since there were no public warehouses like those for tobacco. This was recognized early in the history

---

153. James Davidson to Neil Jamieson, February 9, 1765, ibid., V, p. 964.

154. Archd. Omey to Neil Jamieson, December 12, 1767, ibid., VIII, p. 1848.

of the trade as a limiting factor. Francis Jerdone pointed

out in 1739 that a purchase of 2,000 bushels of wheat was

"as much as I have Convenient house Room for."[155] It was

necessary for large dealers like Jamieson to have a fleet

of river craft to transport the produce to their warehouses

in Norfolk. Adam Fleming told Jamieson in 1770 that two

sellers of wheat in the Cabin Point area "Grumbels a good

deale and Says they wont Kepe it much Longer."[156] In another

year, he reported: "There is aboute 1000 Bushels Corn that

Lyes upon the River at different places that I must take

away before this Month is out Therefore youll please send

up a Vessel for it."[157] In the winter of 1773, Fleming ex-

plained that 1,200 bushels of the wheat which he had pur-

chased "must be taken away as Soon as possibel as it lys in

the peopels way."[158]

Maintenance of a standard of quality was a difficult

---

155. Francis Jerdone to Neil Buchanan, August 8, 1739, Letterbook of Francis Jerdone, I.

156. Adam Fleming to Neil Jamieson, January 15, 1770, Papers of Neil Jamieson, XI, p. 2429.

157. Adam Fleming to James Glassford, March 1, 1772, ibid., XV, p. 3311.

158. Adam Fleming to Neil Jamieson, December 11, 1773, ibid., XIX, p. 4306.

problem. Legislation in the 1740's and '50's provided for
the inspection of flour, meat, pitch and tar, and lumber,
but the methods of enforcement were inadequate. In 1772,
though, an act was passed providing for more effective regulation of the flour trade. The law required flour to be
graded and sold in casks of a specified size, marked with
the maker's name and the weight of the flour.[159] Buyers
usually were able to judge the quality of a shipment by
examining a sample. In purchasing flour, Arthur Morson of
Falmouth told Jamieson that he never examined "above two
Barrells of a Waggon Load when they are all one mans make
& manufactored at the same Mill." If the merchant's inspection did not detect bad produce, "whatever loss had
happend must be sustaind by the Store here."[160]

Methods of purchasing produce from the growers
were similar to those in the tobacco trade. In the earlier
years of the eighteenth century, barter seems to have been
fairly extensive. Francis Jerdone spoke in 1739 of allowing

---

159. Thomson, "Merchant in Virginia," pp. 126-130.

160. Arthur Morson to Neil Jamieson, June 15, 1771,
Papers of Neil Jamieson, XIV, p. 3089. Philadelphia merchants sometimes complained about the quality of wheat and
the shortness of measures in Virginia, according to Jensen,
Maritime Commerce of Colonial Philadelphia, p. 77.

"a Bus[hel of] salt for one of wheat" in making a purchase of 1,000 bushels.[161]  However, by 1771, as Robert Pleasants pointed out, wheat on the James River was "almost a ready money article."[162]  Arthur Morson reported from Falmouth in 1773:

> I have hardly received a hundred Bushells of wheat yet but I expect 4 or 500 Bushells, the price now given is 4/6 half goods half Cash....Most of our Corn Sellers want money for their Corn however I expect to pick up a little for Goods and debts say One hundred Barrells between this & March.[163]

Because of the growing centralization of the produce trade at Norfolk, the major interest of country dealers lay in the going price of commodities at that port.  These communications from Matthias Ellegood of Pasquotank County are representative of inquiries from Virginia and North Carolina storekeepers:  "I do Entend in to See & Talk with you Concerning the Prices of Produce in this Country and see what Prices you think would or may Suit to give for Each Kind" and "Inform me by him [the bearer of this note]

---

161.  Francis Jerdone to Neil Buchanan, [September] 20, 1739, Letterbook of Francis Jerdone, I.

162.  Robert Pleasants to "Brother," December 17, 1771, Letterbook of Robert Pleasants.

163.  Arthur Morson to Neil Jamieson, November 20, 1773, Papers of Neil Jamieson, XIX, p. 4277.

whether you think Pork and Corn will have a high Price this year with you or not."[164]

But the Meetings of Merchants at Williamsburg played a role in pricing of grain and other produce similar to that in the decentralized tobacco trade. James Robinson pointed out in 1774 that the agents of Philadelphia merchants were "doing a Great deal of business at our Generall Courts."[165] James Glassford, Jamieson's partner in Norfolk, mentioned on at least one occasion price quotations on wheat at Williamsburg.[166] Robert Pleasants wrote in 1772 that "there is yet no price fix'd or any agreem[en]t about it [i.e., corn] but I suppose that will be done at the present meeting in Wmsburg."[167] A year later, Robert Carter related that "the price of wheat is yet undetermined" because the previous Meeting "did not fix the Value." He described Williamsburg

---

164. Matthias Ellegood to Neil Jamieson, November 14 and November 24, 1764, ibid., IV, pp. 881 and 886.

165. James Robinson to William Cuninghame & Company, February 7, 1774, Letterbook of William Cuninghame & Company, II.

166. Adam Fleming to James Glassford, December 4, 1772, Papers of Neil Jamieson, XVI, p. 3673. Fleming stated: "I Observe what you Say [in your latest letter] with Regard to wheat Selling 4/ in Wmbs...."

167. Robert Pleasants to "Brother," May 10, 1772, Letterbook of Robert Pleasants.

as "the great Mart for Wheat."[168]

## C.  THE TRADE IN IMPORTED GOODS

The distribution of imported goods in the colony was closely connected with the collection of tobacco and other commodities for export, in that the same institutions performed both functions.  Successful operations of exporters thus depended upon the proper selection and pricing of goods and commodities imported from abroad, so that they might build up a clientele among planters and farmers.  Indeed, one Glasgow merchant maintained that the profit on the sale of goods made it worthwhile to purchase tobacco in Virginia even when the commodity was sold at a nominal loss in Scotland.[169]  James Robinson calculated that the Cuninghame store at Rocky Ridge would lose almost £2 per hogshead on 200 hogsheads exported in 1771-1772, unless, he told his storekeeper, "you Sell more goods and at a greater advance."[170]

---

168.  Robert Carter to Robert Prentis, July 24, 1773; Carter to Col. Warner Lewis, August 30, 1773, Letterbook of Robert Carter (Duke University).

169.  Coulter, "Virginia Merchant," pp. 106-108.

170.  James Robinson to John Turner, April 11, 1772, Letterbook of William Cuninghame & Company, I.

The greater the assortment of European merchandise and West Indian commodities, the more likely was the store to attract customers. One factor, who operated a store at Leedstown, complained to his employer: "I hope you do not intend these goods as a proper supply of Fall Goods for your store; if you do, your Customers must go to some other Merchant."[171] The manager of the Glassford store in Mecklenburg County wrote to Jamieson that the "Many stores in the neighborhood...oblidge me to keep a better assortment both of European & West India Goods than what I would else do." He urged Jamieson to send him the best quality of sugar available, "which will stop the murmering of the people."[172]

Storekeepers in the Cuninghame chain, like those in other stores, bore the responsibility of making out the schemes, or orders, of goods, on the basis of expected demand. They were advised by the chief factor to specify precisely "the Quality and price of the most minute articles." When the Cuninghame firm shipped gun powder from a new source of supply in Britain, the manager of the Fauquier store was

---

171. Thomas Jett to Perkins, Buchanan & Brown, November 5, 1772, Jerdone Papers.

172. Ebenezer Machang to Jamieson, June 13, 1770, Papers of Neil Jamieson.

told to have it "tryd by some Person you Can Confide in and advise of its Character that we may regulate our next Orders Accordingly."[173]

Goods were generally priced in local currency in terms of an advance over sterling costs; that is, goods which cost £100 sterling in Britain would be priced at £175 Virginia currency if the advance was 75 per cent. This advance covered the difference between local currency and sterling, freight, handling and other charges, and a profit to the merchandizer. Thus, the prices of imported goods rose and fell with the rate of sterling exchange.[174] Also, the advance was likely to be higher in areas where there were few competitors. For example, one factor in King and Queen County complained to his principals that he could not retail at as high an advance as a store maintained by the same company at another location because of the vigorous competition from a neighboring establishment.[175]

The storekeeper had some leeway in the pricing of

---

173. James Robinson to John Turner, April 22, 1769, Letterbook of William Cuninghame & Company, I.

174. See below, Chapter III, for a discussion of the market for sterling exchange in Virginia.

175. Robinson Daingerfield to John & William McCall, July 14, 1768, Caroline County Appeals.

individual articles. As Robinson pointed out to the new

manager of a Cuninghame store, "great regard must be had to

the quality of the goods; as you Know goods of the same

Cost will not Allways bear the same advance."[176] Some

stores used symbols in their invoices to indicate the ster-

ling price of goods, so that the seller might have an advan-

tage in bargaining for as high a price as possible over

original costs. In a post-Revolutionary debt case, a former

clerk in a Scottish store in King and Queen County stated

that "the mark used...for expressing the Cost of the Goods

was the Letters m, o, r, d, i, c, a, e, u, s to represent

the figures 1, 2, 3, 4, 5, 6, 7, 8, 9, 0."[177]

A practice followed by some stores was to mark

up the sterling costs on the invoice. For example, one

customer agreed in 1761 to take goods from a King and Queen

County store at an advance of 85 per cent. Afterwards, he

became convinced that the items which he had purchased had

been "advanced at least 25 per cent on the first Cost [in

Britain] before the advance agreed on was Superadded." Thus,

---

176. James Robinson to William Cuninghame, October 8, 1771, Letterbook of William Cuninghame & Company, I.

177. Deposition of Benjamin Pollard, Caroline County Appeals.

he was in reality paying a mark-up of over 110 per cent instead of 85 per cent. The factor at this store justified this policy by maintaining that customers were more concerned with the rate of advance than with the sterling cost of goods. Thus, to raise the latter would be less likely to result in the loss of sales than to increase the former. In reply to a later request of this factor to raise further the invoice price before the goods were shipped, the Glasgow firm pointed out that "you can Judge better how to make any additional advance in the country than we can here."[178]

Judged by modern standards of business conduct, some of these practices in pricing goods would seem to lend substance to the claim of the planters that the merchants "charged exorbitant profits for the goods and wares given in exchange" for tobacco.[179] Indeed, traders sometimes entered into agreements to raise the advance on goods retailed in the stores. For example, David Ross wrote from Petersburg in 1772 that "the Merchants at this place and Blandford are to meet on Friday afternoon to deliberate on the present

178. Robinson Daingerfield to John & William McCall, July 8, 1762; John & William McCall to Robinson Daingerfield, March 8, 1763, Caroline County Appeals.

179. Cabell, "Report on the Post Revolutionary History of Agriculture in Virginia," p. 151.

situation of their Trade, and I believe it will be the un-
animous opinion that the advance on retail shall be raised
to 75 per Cent, if the Merchants up James River are agree-
able."[130]

However, this was not an era when merchandizers
adhered to a one-price policy in selling their goods.  Few
would have agreed with Quaker George Fox that haggling over
individual deals was both deceitful and time-wasting.[181]
Charging what the traffic would bear continued for many
years to be the practice in retailing.  High profit margins
on goods did not end with the American Revolution.  In the
early nineteenth century, wholesalers generally charged a
mark-up of 100 to 150 per cent of the original cost of merchandize, to which southern retailers added a similar
advance.[182]  Thus, the high prices of imported goods resulted perhaps not so much from deceit and collusion among
sellers as from the high costs of marketing in a rural
economy.

---

180.  David Ross to John Hook, September 16, 1772,
Papers of John Hook.

181.  Ralph M. Hower, History of Macy's of New York,
1858-1919 (Cambridge: Harvard University Press, 1943),
pp. 89-90.

182.  Lewis E. Atherton, The Southern Country Store,
1800-1860 (Baton Rouge: Louisiana State University Press,
1949), p. 170.

## D.   PLANTERS AND MERCHANTS

Whether Virginians would have received greater benefits from some alternative system of marketing agricultural commodities is, of course, impossible to determine. Even the ultimate impact of British enumeration, the requirement that all tobacco be exported to Great Britain, is an unsettled question.  One recent writer has emphasized the advantage to Virginia tobacco producers of "the great central marketing machinery" which was created by British merchants, in part because they were assured protection against foreign competition in the American tobacco trade.[183]

That "outsiders" to Virginia society - that is, English and Scottish merchants - dominated both the consignment

---

183.   Dickerson, The Navigation Acts and the American Revolution, pp. 33-39.  On the other hand, Lawrence A. Harper, "The Effect of the Navigation Acts on the Thirteen Colonies" in The Era of the American Revolution, ed. Richard B. Morris (New York: Columbia University Press, 1939), points to the steady decline in the percentage of American tobacco exports going to Great Britain after independence as evidence that Britain was not a natural entrepôt for American tobacco.  However, the tobacco industry in the United States underwent major changes in the late eighteenth and early nineteenth centuries, in geographical areas of production and in types of leaf grown.  These changes, as well as the impact of the European wars on established marketing channels, should perhaps be taken into consideration.  See Gray, Agriculture in the Southern United States to 1860, II, 752-778.

system and the store trade has been attributed by at least

one writer to "the failure of the planters to think like

capitalists or to live like prudent speculators."[184]  Yet

even the small producer invested capital in land, labor

(slaves), and equipment to produce a commodity for a specu-

lative market.  The land speculation of the larger planters

as well as the trading and manufacturing enterprises of men

like Robert Carter attest to the business-mindedness of a

significant portion of the tobacco producers.[185]  However,

some question might be raised about the extent to which

planters, when they were faced with adverse markets or

with declining yields due to soil exhaustion, understood

the impersonal action of the organized market which deter-

mined prices, paid for tobacco and charged for goods, "with-

out reference to their needs or their deserts, without pre-

judice or favor."[186]  Under these circumstances, it was easy

to transfer the blame for economic misfortune to the mercantile

---

184.  Price, "The French Farmers-General in the Chesapeake," p. 152.

185.  See Louis Morton, Robert Carter of Nomini Hall
(Williamsburg: Colonial Williamsburg, 1941).

186.  F. L. Nussbaum, A History of the Economic Institutions of Modern Europe (New York: F. S. Crofts & Company,
1935), p. 247.

community, many of whose members remained aloof from the general population of the colony.

Although planters were themselves businessmen producing commodities for a market, they would likely have agreed with Francis Parkman's later comment that "business swallows much that is noble,"[187] at least when practiced by the professional trader. Merchant Charles Steuart of Norfolk testified to the hostility between producer and middleman when he complained in 1751 that the planters in the Virginia legislature "in their great Wisdoms think fit to lay the Burthen for the support of [the provincial] Government upon Trade, not considering that they are [as] nearly concerned in the Increase or decay of it."[188]

---

187. Quoted by E. N. Saveth, "What Historians Teach About Business," Fortune (April, 1952).

188. Charles Steuart to Walter Tullideph, September 23, 1751, Letterbook of Charles Steuart, I.

III


MONEY, CREDIT, AND STERLING EXCHANGE


Money and credit were, of course, essential to the conduct of business in eighteenth-century Virginia. Like other colonies, though, the Old Dominion suffered from a shortage of currency to provide a medium of exchange. As an underdeveloped area, Virginia was dependent upon Great Britain for capital to finance trade and economic development.

This chapter discusses in turn the currency problem and expedients devised to deal with it, the operation of the credit system, and the mechanism of the sterling exchange market which facilitated the financing of the trans-Atlantic movement of goods and commodities. As indicated earlier, it was in the functioning of the financial system that the Williamsburg Meeting of Merchants played a key role in the economic life of the colony.

## A.   THE CURRENCY PROBLEM

Throughout the colonial period, the British government never provided specifically for a currency for the pro-
vinces.  Furthermore, Great Britain prohibited the expor-
tation of its own currency to the colonies and forbade the
establishment of mints there.  Another element of the problem
was the adverse balance of payments of the colonies, which
resulted in a drain of some of the available supply of specie,
particularly during trade depressions.[1]  The upshot was a
shortage of currency and the separation of the two principal
functions of money - to serve as a standard of value and
as a medium of exchange.[2]  Virginia, like other colonies,
used the British monetary system of pounds, shillings, and
pence as a measure of value.  But the medium of exchange
consisted of many different kinds of "money."

Currency in Circulation.  From an early date, the

---

1.   Curtis P. Nettels, The Money Supply of the American
Colonies Before 1720 (Madison: n.p., 1934), pp. 162-178.
E. James Ferguson, "Currency Finance: An Interpretation of
Colonial Monetary Practices," William and Mary Quarterly,
3d ser., X (1953), 153-180.

2.   For a discussion of the function of money in exchange economy, see Lester V. Chandler, An Introduction to
Monetary Theory (New York: Harper & Brothers, 1940), pp. 1-20.

Spanish "piece of eight" and the Portuguese "joe" became
the basis of the circulating coinage in the colonies.  These
silver and gold coins, obtained largely through trade with
the West Indies, were valued in terms of the English monetary system.  But, because of the adverse balance of payments, these coins were often used to pay foreign debts,
thereby reducing the amount of coinage serving as a medium
of exchange in the colonies.[3]

In order to attract hard money and to prevent
the drain of the supply of coins, each of the colonies in
the late seventeenth and early eighteenth centuries enacted
laws to raise the legal tender value of foreign coins.  The
assumption was that if a coin was worth more in America than
in England, it would remain in the colony.  Thus, each colony set its own value on the Spanish "piece of eight,"
according to its own trading needs.  Among the colonies,
the value of the Spanish "piece of eight," or milled dollar,
which was worth four shillings six pence in sterling money,
ranged from four shillings eight pence to eight shillings.[4]

---

3.  Nettels, Money Supply of the American Colonies,
pp. 230-232.

4.  Edward Channing, A History of the United States
(New York: Macmillan Company, 1930-1938), II, 497-500.

After 1727, the official value of a Spanish dollar containing 386.8 grains of pure silver was fixed in Virginia at six shillings.[5] Table XI shows the official value of other coins in circulation there during the eighteenth-century.

Users of coins had to examine each one received in order to detect variations in weight and fineness. Original errors committed at the mint were compounded by clipping and sweating, or removing part of the bullion content.[6] The author of a treatise on the currencies of the colonies advised American merchants to follow the European "Practice of the old Traders and established Houses to be continually weighing most of the Money that passes into their Hands."[7] Robert Carter Nicholas, Treasurer of the provincial government, wrote to John Norton in 1769, to order a set of "Money Scales..., one of the best Sort of Hyrdostatick Balances,

---

5. William Z. Ripley, The Financial History of Virginia, 1609-1776 (New York: Columbia College, 1893), pp. 130-133. Charles J. Bullock, Essays on the Monetary History of the United States (New York: Macmillan Company, 1900), pp. 17, 20. The price of gold was fixed in Virginia in 1700 at 5 shillings per pennyweight, with twenty pennyweight equivalent to one ounce.

6. Ray A. Foulke, The Sinews of American Commerce (New York: Dun & Bradstreet, 1941), p. 32.

7. J. Wright, The American Negotiator, or the Various Currencies of the British Colonies in America, 3d ed. (London: J. Smith, 1765), p. lxxvi.

TABLE XI: OFFICIAL VALUE OF FOREIGN COINS IN CIRCULATION
         IN VIRGINIA IN THE EIGHTEENTH CENTURY.


| Spanish Coins | Rating in Virginia Currency |
|---|---|
| *Milled dollar (piece of Eight) (8 reals) | 6 shillings |
| Half dollar (4 reals) | 3 shillings |
| Quarter dollar (2 reals) (Pistareen) | 1 shilling 6 pence |
| Eighth dollar (1 real) | 9 pence |

| Portuguese Coins | |
|---|---|
| Johannes ("Joe") (16 Spanish dollars) | 96 shillings |
| Half-Joe | 48 shillings |
| Quarter-Joe | 24 shillings |
| Moidore | 36 shillings |

| French | |
|---|---|
| Pistol (4 Spanish dollars) | 23-24 shillings |


*The milled dollar was rated in Sterling at 4 shillings
6 pence.




Source:   Edward Channing, A History of the United States
          (New York: Macmillan Company, 1930-1938), II,
          498-499.

TABLE XII:   OFFICIAL VALUES OF CURRENCY IN THE COLONIES
             IN THE EIGHTEENTH CENTURY

| Colony | Value of Spanish milled dollar in local currency | Ratio of £ Local currency to Sterling £ (£ sterling = 100) |
|---|---|---|
| Virginia | 6 shillings | 75 |
| North Carolina | 8 shillings | 56 1/4 |
| South Carolina | 4 shillings 8 pence | 90 |
| Georgia | 4 shillings 8 pence | 90 |
| Maryland | 7 shillings 6 pence | 60 |
| Delaware | 7 shillings 6 pence | 60 |
| Pennsylvania | 7 shillings 6 pence | 60 |
| New Jersey | 7 shillings 6 pence | 60 |
| New York | 8 shillings | 56 1/4 |
| Connecticut | 6 shillings | 75 |
| Rhode Island | 6 shillings | 75 |
| Massachusetts | 6 shillings | 75 |
| New Hampshire | 6 shillings | 75 |

Source: Edward Channing, A History of the United States
        (New York: Macmillan Company, 1930-1938), II, 499n.

for determining the fineness of Gold & Silver with the most
approved Treatise upon the Subject;" he explained that "there
is a good deal of base coin circulating amongst us & I must
be a little upon my Guard."[8] A few years later, Nicholas
pointed out that "our Gold & Silver is not free from Counterfeits, I have too much Reason to fear there is a good deal
of each in the Circle."[9]

Although there were small coins in the Spanish
system, the lowest denomination in general circulation in
the colonies was the one real piece, equivalent to nine
pence in Virginia currency.[10] The colony as early as 1642
attempted to mint copper coins to meet the need for a sub-
sidiary coinage, but the plan failed, as did later ones in
1726, 1769, and 1772.[11] Robert Carter Nicholas described
"the inconveniences Many Parts of this Country labour under
for want of a small Species of Coin in the ordinary Course

---

8. R. C. Nicholas to John Norton, November 4, 1769,
Frances N. Mason, ed., John Norton & Sons: Merchants of
London and Virginia (Richmond: Dietz Press, 1937), p. 109.

9. R. C. Nicholas to John Norton & Son, March 17, 1773,
ibid., p. 307.

10. Nettels, Money Supply of the American Colonies,
p. 172.

11. Ripley, Financial History of Virginia, pp. 111-114,
131.

of Business."[12]

Commodity Money. From an early date, most colonies used certain commodities as money to overcome the
shortage of coin. Commodity money differed from simple
barter when the colonial legislature decreed that a certain
product should be received in payment of taxes and other
public debts. Those who accepted a quantity of a commodity
as money did so in the expectation that they could use it
to purchase some other article.[13]

In Virginia, tobacco was accepted in payment of
taxes and used to pay salaries of government officials and
Anglican clergymen. However, tobacco, like other commodities in use as money in other colonies, possessed basic de-
fects both as a medium of exchange and as a standard of
value. The problems of transporting and storing commodities
which are bulky and heavy in relation to their value are
obvious. As one writer has pointed out, it is difficult
to conceive of "'gallant young Virginians hastening to the
water-side, each carrying a bundle of the best tobacco under

12. R. C. Nicholas to John Norton, Nov. 30, 1772,
Mason, John Norton & Sons, p. 287.

13. Nettels, Money Supply of the American Colonies,
p. 209.

his arm' in order to purchase a wife," when "the burden of these ardent lovers would have amounted to above two tons."[14] Equally serious in its effect on the use of tobacco as money was the fluctuation in its price, as determined by the forces of supply and demand. Also, wide differences in quality made difficult the use of commodities as a common measure of value, since the person tendering a commodity as money was tempted to deliver his most inferior product.[15]

The inspection system, established in 1730, removed some of the difficulties inherent in the use of tobacco as money. As indicated in a previous chapter, the act of 1730 established a minimum standard of quality. The public warehouses made storage more convenient. Most significant, the notes issued for merchantable tobacco passed in local exchange and for payment of taxes. Tobacco notes were declared "to be current & paiable in all tobacco paiments...within the county" where the commodity was inspected and stored, "or in any other county adjacent thereto, and not separated by any of the great rivers or bay."[16]

---

14. Ripley, Financial History of Virginia, p. 146.

15. Nettels, Money Supply of the American Colonies, pp. 210-214.

16. William W. Hening, ed., The Statutes at Large:

Initially, only transfer notes, representing bulk deposits
of tobacco, were accepted as legal tender. However, after
1748, crop notes, issued against specified hogsheads of tobacco, also could be used to make payments of legal obligations on the same terms.[17]

On the whole, the system of tobacco notes, which
represented the highest development of commodity money in
the colonies, worked well enough to retard the introduction
of a genuine paper currency in Virginia. Long-term changes
in the value of tobacco notes, based upon tobacco prices,
were more moderate than the fluctuations in the currencies
of colonies which had issued large volumes of paper money
during the first half of the eighteenth century. But short-
term fluctuations resulted during years of poor crops.[18]
This was the case in 1758, when drought brought a sharp increase of tobacco prices. This led to the Two Penny Acts,
which commuted tobacco payments to cash at a rate of 16

---

being a Collection of All the Laws of Virginia (Richmond,
1810-1823), IV, 252.

17. Ripley, Financial History of Virginia, pp. 150-151.

18. Leslie Van Horn Brock, "Currency of the American
Colonies, 1700-1764: A Study in Colonial Finances and Im-
perial Relations" (Unpublished Ph.D. dissertation, University of Michigan, 1941), pp. 13-14.

shillings 8 pence per hundred pounds, when the market price
stood at 27 shillings. The basic problem derived from the
dual nature of tobacco as a staple and as money. As one
writer has noted, "an appreciating currency works hardships
on debtors no less than a depreciating currency does on
creditors."[19]

Paper Money. All of the thirteen colonies issued
paper money during the eighteenth century, with varying de-
grees of success. Massachusetts was the first to experiment in supplementing the hard money available, with its
initial issue of 1691, and Virginia was one of the last in
1755.[20]

Although administrative and legal details varied
in many ways among paper money issues, there were bascially
two methods followed by the different colonies in their
emissions. One was the land-bank system, in which an
agency of the provincial government created paper money to
lend to its citizens on the security of their land or other
real estate. This method was particularly successful in

---

19. Ibid., pp. 510-512.

20. Nettels, Money Supply of the American Colonies,
pp. 250-277.

the middle colonies, where the volume of paper issued was moderate and the security was profitable agricultural land. Inflation resulted in other colonies from excessive amounts issued.[21]

Virginia utilized the alternative system of issuing bills of credit, or treasury notes, based on future tax receipts. The occasion in Virginia, as in the initial issues of bills of credit in most other colonies, resulted from war-time financial need.[22] As was the case in Massachusetts in the 1690's, the problem was more a shortage of cash in the provincial treasury than a general shortage of money in the colony.[23] The legislature, faced in 1755 with the necessity of raising money for the war with France, levied £20,000 in extra taxes. Rather than follow the usual procedure of increasing the levies payable in tobacco, the Assembly decided to meet the immediate crisis by authorizing the issue of £20,000 in treasury notes to be redeemed the following year with the proceeds of the tax levy. The bills, declared to be legal tender for all debts except

---

21. Theodore Thayer, "The Land-Bank System in the American Colonies," Journal of Economic History, XIII (1953), 145-159.

22. Ferguson, "Currency Finance," pp. 160, 171-173.

23. Nettels, Money Supply of the American Colonies, p. 255.

the quit rents, bore interest at 5 per cent.[24] Essentially,

the bills were promissory notes issued by the government,

used to pay suppliers of provisions and others to whom the

government owed money. It was expected then that the bills

would be withdrawn from circulation as citizens presented

them to the Treasury in payment of taxes and other obligations

due to the government. The basic security was the fund as-

signed to redeem the bills. The notes would depreciate,

or lose value, unless holders maintained faith that future

governments would have the ability and the will to collect

taxes of an amount equal to withdraw the money from circu-

lation. If the quantity of money outstanding exceeded the

requirements of trade at existing price levels, depreciation

would take place regardless of guarantees.[25]

It soon became apparent that further financing

was needed for the war effort, as a special session of the

Assembly in the summer of 1755 authorized another issue of

£40,000 to run for four years and to be covered by special

taxes. Indeed, so successful were these first two flota-

tions that there was considerable backing for a land bank

which would issue £200,000 in paper money on the security

---

24.  Ripley, <u>Financial History of Virginia</u>, p. 154.

25.  Ferguson, "Currency Finance," p. 173.

of real estate.[26] Merchant Charles Steuart believed that this issue of paper money would "enable people to pay their debts, & put an end to [protested?] bills."[27]

No land-bank scheme ever succeeded in Virginia, but before the war ended in 1763, the provincial government had made fourteen emissions of bills of credit, totalling almost £540,000. As shown in Table XIII (following p. 132), the largest single issue was that of April, 1757, for almost £100,000. Following the practice of other colonies, Virginia paid no interest except on the notes of the first four issues.[28] Three further emissions, amounting to almost £77,000, were made in the post-war period, principally to cover losses of tobacco in the public warehouses.[29] These later issues were payable for public debts but were not a

---

26. Ripley, Financial History of Virginia, pp. 154-155. In the 1770's, two acts to establish land banks were passed by the House of Burgesses but annulled by the Council, Ferguson, "Currency Finance," p. 178.

27. Charles Steuart to William Bowden, date torn [between October 15-November 20, 1755], Letterbook of Charles Steuart (Historical Society of Pennsylvania), I.

28. Brock, "Currency of the American Colonies," p. 475.

29. Ripley, Financial History of Virginia, pp. 161-162. The provincial government was required to pay for tobacco stored in public warehouses and lost as a result of natural catastrophe, such as the floods which occured in the spring of 1771.

legal tender, since Parliament in 1764 prohibited the colonies to issue paper money as legal tender.[30]

The treasury notes were gradually withdrawn from
circulation in the 1760's as they were tendered in tax payments.  Of the £539,962 authorized during the war, only
£206,757 was in circulation in 1767.  Notes totalling
£103,000 were still unredeemed in 1771, two years after
the date for final retirement of the last war issue.[31]

Virginia escaped the worst effects of inflation
which resulted in other colonies from excessive volume of
paper currency, but the colony experienced some of the
problems of dealing with fiat money.  Space does not permit
here an elaboration of the arguments advanced by protago-
nists in the controversy over the propriety of bills of
credit.  However, once paper money was in circulation as
part of the colony's money supply, confidence in the public
officials responsible for its administration was essential
to the maintenance of its value.  Not only was there the
temptation of personal gain for public officials in charge

30.  "Paper Money in Virginia," William and Mary Quarterly, 1st. ser., XX (1912), 228.  Brock, "Currency of the
American Colonies," pp. 507-508.

31.  "Paper Money in Virginia," p. 228.

of paper money,[32] but there was also possibility of manipulation of currency for political advantage. The "Robinson
affair" in the mid-1760's underscored the problem of the
public official in a position where he could alter the economic fortunes of many in the colony.[33]

John Robinson, prominent member of the Virginia
gentry, had "wielded more power than any other man in the
Colony" for a quarter of a century as Speaker of the House
of Burgesses and Treasurer of the province. Upon Robinson's
death in 1766, it was discovered that he had made private
emissions to hard-pressed planters of more than £100,000 of
treasury bills which were presented for redemption. Robinson
had seen the deflationary effects of the withdrawal from
circulation of the war-time paper money; thus, he sought to
ease the shock by unofficially re-issuing the treasury bills

---

32. Land-banks, which were public institutions, faced
this kind of difficulty in colonies where they were established. In one case, the director of the Pennsylvania land-
bank reported that a large sum of money belonging to the
loan office was stolen from his home, but it was believed
that the director had invented the robbery story to hide the
fact that he had used the money himself. Thayer, "The Land-
Bank System," p. 158.

33. David J. Mays, Edmund Pendleton, 1721-1803: A Biography (Cambridge: Harvard University Press, 1952), I,
174-223, is the most complete account available of this
affair.

which had been slated by law for retirement. "He could burn the paper money and bankrupt his friends, or ignore the law and make the paper available to those in desperate need."[34] The largest single beneficiary of Robinson's largesse was William Byrd III, who owed £14,921. Members of the Council had borrowed collectively nearly £15,600, those of the House more than £37,000. Robinson's political friends generally were favored, although opponents would have received loans "had they asked for it, of course, not solely because that would have been good politics from Robinson's standpoint, but because of his genuine goodness of heart."[35]

Another major problem was that of counterfeiting, particularly of the issues of 1769 and 1771. So serious was the dislocation of the currency system that the Governor called a special session of the Assembly in 1773 to authorize a loan of over £36,000 for the rapid retirement of the old notes.[36] One merchant referred to the "Stagnation of Business occasion'd by the great quantities of very ingenious forgeries of our paper Cur[ren]cy. lately discover'd to be

---

34. Mays, *Pendleton*, I, 175.

35. *Ibid.*, I, 184.

36. Ripley, *Financial History of Virginia*, p. 161.

in Circulation."[37]  Many lost heavily by the counterfeit

bills.  As a Richmond storekeeper put it, "the trading part

of this Country have suffered much lately by some very in-

genious counterfeits of the paper money at present in circu-

lation.  I loose about forty pounds by it, and am most thank-

full that I have escaped so well."[38]  So clever was the

printing of the bogus bills, according to one observer, that

"the distance of the White lines in the paper is the Only

way they can be discovered."[39]  Significantly, some merchants

suspected a repetition of something like the "Robinson

affair."  "I'm of opinion if ever there is a discovery,"

maintained  James Parker, wealthy Norfolk merchant, "that

some of the Great needy Ones have got hold of the Old Types."[40]

In spite of these problems, the paper money

---

37.  Robert Pleasants to Joshua Fisher & Sons, March 12,
1773, Letterbook of Robert Pleasants (College of William
and Mary).

38.  R. Donald to Charles Steuart, February 10, 1773,
Charles Steuart Papers (National Library of Scotland), MS.
5028, p. 29.

39.  James Parker to Charles Steuart, February 20, 1773,
ibid., MS. 5028, p. 32.

40.  James Parker to Charles Steuart, February 20, 1773,
ibid., MS. 5028, p. 32.  The "Great needy Ones" obviously
referred to the same group of planters who had benefitted
from Speaker Robinson's private emissions of paper money.

experiment was on the whole successful in Virginia.  Robert
Carter Nicholas, who succeeded Robinson as Treasurer of the
colony, maintained in 1773 that "for many Years...the Paper
Money was generally preferred to Gold or Silver,...and this,
even under the supposed Disadvantage of its not being a
legal Tender, which surely must be considered by every impartial Person as a proof of its Goodness."[41]  Nicholas
probably reflected the attitude of many Virginians when he
stated: "I am sure a moderate quantity of it [i.e., paper
money] would be extremely useful in transacting the Business of this Country,...[but] I can say with great Truth
that I shou'd never desire to see any Paper Money if we
could possibly do without it."[42]  William Allason of Falmouth wrote, when money was scarce in 1767, that "we shall
in some time be as fond of having our Assembly authorized
by Parliament, to Emitt more paper Currency, as we was some
time ago of preventing it."[43]  Although much of the historical

---

41.  Robert C. Nicholas to Purdie and Dixon, September 22,
1773, in "Paper Money in Virginia," p. 256.

42.  Robert C. Nicholas to John Norton & Sons, March 17,
1773, Mason, John Norton & Sons, p. 307.

43.  William Allason to Robert Allason, October 29, 1767,
Letterbook of William Allason, Allason Papers (Virginia
State Library).

writing has emphasized the use of paper money as a device by which colonial debtors could reduce their real debt load, bills of credit actually provided the colonies an expedient to meet financial emergencies and a circulating medium to supplement specie.[44]

Substitutes for Money. Because of the lack of an adequate supply of money, businessmen turned to a number of devices to make transactions without using currency.[45] The private sector as well as the public sector developed expedients to meet the problem of the shortage of currency.

Some kind of barter was used in many dealings. For example, William Holt reported in 1768 that "the most that I have done is in the Barter way. Rum at 2/6 for Corn

---

44. Brock, "Currency of the American Colonies," p. 557. See Ferguson, "Currency Finance," pp. 153-157, for a brief review of the historiography of paper money in the colonial period.

45. See W. T. Baxter, House of Hancock: Business in Boston, 1724-1775 (Cambridge, Mass.: Harvard University Press, 1945), pp. 16-34, for the similar ways in which Massachusetts merchants conducted "Trade Without Money." Some of the terms used here are those applied by Baxter to the Hancocks' trade.

at 10/."[46]  Essentially the trade of the tobacco-purchasing

stores was based on barter, as planters exchanged their to-

bacco for merchandise.  However, this was more than simple

barter, since the planter usually did not bring a quantity

of tobacco to the store each time he wished to acquire an

item of merchandise.  The hogshead was too large a unit for

this purpose.  Furthermore, the planter often needed imported

goods at a time when tobacco was not available.  Thus, there

developed a system of "bookkeeping barter" or a "two-way

flow of goods and services."  The planter withdrew merchan-

dise from the store as needed and settled his "running charge

account" annually by presenting the storekeeper with to-

bacco notes.  No actual cash might change hands, but both

sides of the transaction were rated in money values.[47]

---

46.  William Holt to William Palfrey, February 26, 1768,
Palfrey Papers (Harvard College Library).

47.  Calvin B. Coulter, "The Virginia Merchant" (Unpublished Ph.D. dissertation, Princeton University, 1944),
pp. 105-106.  The use of English money as a measure of
value was characteristic in all of the colonies during both
the seventeenth and eighteenth centuries, even where and
when money was not available as a medium of exchange.  For
example, a set of seventeenth-century account books of a
Springfield, Massachusetts, merchant, in the possession of
the Connecticut Valley Historical Society, show that "each
item, including labor, was assessed a monetary value."  The
study of these records is described in a story in the New
York Times, July 1, 1956.

Francis Jerdone used this system of bookkeeping barter to pay his shirtmaker. According to a ledger entry of April, 1751, Jerdone owed £6.10.6 to Miss Jean Ansell of Yorktown for "making & mending my shirts to the last of this month." As payment for these services, he made the following entries in Miss Ansell's account:

1751
| | | |
|---|---|---|
| April 4 | To: 1 lb Bohea tea 7/  1 1/4 yd<br>fine muzlin @8/ 10/ | £-:17:- |
| May 1 | To: 11 1/2 yds Bed type at 2/4. 26/10:<br>1 pr kid Gloves 3/4 | 1:10:2 |
| June 10 | To: 1 lb Bohea Tea 7/ 1 lb Coffee 2/<br>2 Bed Cords 3/ | -:12:- |
| August 12 | To: 8 lb Cheese @ 7 1/2 5/  1/2 lb<br>Bohea Tea 3/9 | -: 8:9 |
| Sept 3 | To: 1 pr womens worsted hose 4/6.<br>2 3/8 yds fine check @ 2/6 6/ | -:10:6[48] |

To avoid the use of currency, merchants made contracts for the exchange of commodities. For example, Neil Jamieson was a party to this agreement of 1766:

> I agree & Oblige my Self to Deliver to Neil Jamieson & Co. on or before the 1st. of Aug[us]t....a quantity of London Marcell pipe h[ogs]h[ea]d & Barrell white Oak Staves, to be delivered at Norfolk in the time, for which which I am to have Nine pounds p[er] Thousand for Pipe [staves] Six pounds Ten Shillings per [thousand for] h[ogs]h[ea]ds. & Three Pounds Ten shillings p M for Barrells, the whole payable in dry goods out of the said Jamieson & Co. store

---

48. Ledger of Francis Jerdone, 1751-1752 (Colonial Williamsburg), p. 22.

at an Advance of One hundred p[er] c[en]t.[49]
Note again that each side of the transaction was rated in
money, although no cash was involved.

Frequently, third parties were involved in ex-
changes which were made without money. In some of these
instances of triangular transfers of goods, the merchant
was presented, in payment of a debt, with articles for
which he had no immediate need. However, the particular
commodity might be wanted by a third party, who could in
turn tender payment in a more usable form to the original
payee. Other types of transactions were like the one in
which a storekeeper asked Jamieson "to spare me two Barrells
of Pork [as] I am oweing a little Cash and the person will
take Pork."[50]

To summarize briefly, the inadequate supply of
currency resulted in the use of many different mediums of
exchange to serve one measure of value. Although prices
were stated in terms of pounds, shillings, and pence, payments were made in foreign coins, in tobacco notes, in

---

49. H. M. Langston to Neil Jamieson, June 21, 1766,
Papers of Neil Jamieson (Library of Congress), VII, p. 1482.

50. John Smith to Neil Jamieson, April 17, 1769, ibid.,
X, p. 2188.

paper bills, or in one of several methods devised to avoid the use of money altogether.

## B. THE CREDIT SYSTEM

Perhaps the most important point to be made about the credit system in colonial Virginia is the extensive use that was made of it. The basic forces were the need for advances to tide the agricultural producer over until the marketing of his commodities and the shortage of money.

One Virginian commented on the eve of the American Revolution that "credit is a thing so very common here that there is not one person in a hundred who pays the ready money for the goods he takes up to a store."[51] William Reynolds described "the nature of our Trade here" in Virginia as one in which "we are obliged to give extensive credit and a great deal of indulgence especially at first setting out to establish a set of Customers."[52]

---

51. Quoted in Richard B. Sheridan, "The British Credit Crisis of 1772 and the American Colonies," Journal of Economic History, XX (1960), 163.

52. William Reynolds to John Norton, August 10, 1772, Letterbook of William Reynolds (Library of Congress), I.

Operation of the Credit System. At the country
stores throughout the colony, planters and farmers purchased
goods on an unsecured "charge account," with the understanding that the debt would be settled at the end of the
crop year. But to limit credit to twelve months was sometimes a difficult policy to enforce. One Scottish firm
urged its factors in 1765 to "unite in measures for shorting
the Credit to the planters" from the four or five years
which was granted in some cases.[53] Typically, the customer,
when he had discharged his debt for the previous year, began
to accumulate a new one. William Johnston described this
process in the operation of his store in Hanover County in
1739: "So soon as they pay off their old acco[un]t they
emedeatly are in want to run in again and such we look on
as good pay. its true its a great advance of mony but
theirs no  carrying business Such as Yours otherways."[54]

Planters who normally consigned their tobacco to

------

53.   John McCall & James Ritchie & Co. to William Snod-
grass, Robinson Daingerfield, Andrew Crawford, and James
Anderson, February 15, 1765, Caroline County Appeals and
Land Cases, 1787-1807 (Virginia State Library Archives).

54.   William Johnston to Neill Buchanan, October 4, 1739,
Letterbook of Francis Jerdone (College of William and Mary),
I.  Jerdone succeeded Johnston in the operation of this
store after the latter's death in 1741.

be sold in England participated in the credit system in a different way. The bill of exchange drawn on a British merchant against the anticipated proceeds from the sale of the current year's crop was to the consigning planter what open book credit was to the man who dealt exclusively at the country store. Also, the merchants made advances in the form of shipments of goods ordered by the planters. In times of adversity, such as short crops or low prices, the merchants, who maintained close relations with their planter-customers, allowed debts to accumulate and planters to continue to draw bills on the promise of future remittances and shipments. As one writer has put it, the commission merchant "was the planter's personal banker, the source of his credit, and the financier of his plantation and family needs."[55]

Retail stores in Williamsburg, as well as those in rural areas, made most of their sales on credit. Catherine

---

55. Samuel M. Rosenblatt, "The Significance of Credit in the Tobacco Consignment Trade: A Study of John Norton & Sons, 1768-1775," William and Mary Quarterly, 3d ser., XIX (1962), 395. Agents of consignment merchants might also made cash advances on shipments, as William Reynolds observed in 1773: "Their is a Gentleman now soliciting strongly for Consignments to a new house, & at same time offering to advance £5 Sterling a h[ogs]h[ea]d on the shipping." William Reynolds to John Norton, February 8, 1773, Letterbook of William Reynolds, I.

Rathell maintained in 1772 that she sold "for Nothing but redy Cash" in her millinery store, but she had been in Virginia for less than one year when she made this statement and she may have been trying to impress her creditors.[56] Probably typical was the experience of William Prentis and Company, one of the colonial capital's leading stores. The data in Table XIV reflect the importance of credit transactions. The figures on cash and accounts receivable of the company, operated by three generations of the Prentis family, were compiled from balance sheets available for certain years from 1734 to 1775.[57] In 1737, when debts owed to the store amounted to over £2,600, cash on hand was only £10. Similarly, thirty years later accounts receivable stood at over £12,000, but cash on hand consisted of only £70. In only one year for which data are available did cash amount to anywhere near one-third of the combined total of cash on hand and accounts receivable. In most years, debts owed to the store comprised over three-quarters

---

56. Catherine Rathell to John Norton, January 31, 1772, in Mason, John Norton & Sons, pp. 217-218.

57. Prentis Papers (University of Virginia.) The store, which was owned by a group of local investors, operated as William Prentis and Company until the mid-1760's and as John Prentis and Company from then to 1774, when it became Robert Prentis and Company.

of these selected items of current assets.[58]

Virginia merchants and storekeepers, when they imported goods from Great Britain, usually received credit terms of twelve months. Slow communication and transportation necessitated what would be considered today a long period for normal commercial credit. Since the term began from the date of the invoice, when the goods were shipped from London or some other port, and expired when payment was received in Britain, the actual period of use of the credit in America was considerably less than the twelve-month period.[59]

Debts owed to British creditors carried no interest if paid within the time limit originally set, but they incurred a charge of 5 per cent on the unpaid balance after

---

58. The only detailed study of consumer credit in an urban area in the eighteenth century shows that a Philadelphia cabinetmaker made as much as 94 and 99.8 per cent of his total sales on a credit basis in 1774 and 1775. Many colonial businessmen apparently kept records of their credit sales only, but this individual was one of the exceptions who recorded both cash and credit transactions. Wilbur C. Plummer, "Consumer Credit in Colonial Philadelphia," Pennsylvania Magazine of History and Biography, LXVI (1942), 390-391.

59. Arthur S. Williamson, "Credit Relations Between Colonial and English Merchants in the Eighteenth Century" (unpublished Ph.D. dissertation, University of Iowa, 1927), p. 73.

TABLE XIII:   VIRGINIA BILLS OF CREDIT, 1755-1773

| Year | Amount Issued | Date Redeemable |
|------|---------------|-----------------|
| 1755 | £20,000[1] | June 30, 1756 |
| 1755 | 40,000[1] | June 30, 1760 |
| 1756 | 25,000[1] | June 30, 1760 |
| 1756 | 30,000 | June 30, 1760 |
| 1756 | 10,000 | December 15, 1757 |
| 1757 | 80,000 | March 1, 1765 |
| 1757 | 99,962 | March 1, 1765 |
| 1758 | 32,000 | March 1, 1765 |
| 1758 | 57,000 | September 14, 1766 |
| 1759 | 57,000 | April 20, 1768 |
| 1759 | 10,000 | October 20, 1769 |
| 1760 | 20,000 | October 10, 1768 |
| 1760 | 32,000 | October 20, 1769 |
| 1762 | 30,000 | October 20, 1769 |
| 1769 | 10,000[2] | November 20, 1771 |
| 1771 | 30,000[2] | December 10, 1775 |
| 1773 | 36,834[3] | June 1, 1774 |

Total of all issues: £614,796.

1.  Bore 5% interest.
2.  Payable for public debts, but not legal tender.
3.  Payable to "such persons as may be willing to receive
        the same."

Source:   "Paper Money in Virginia,"  William and Mary
        Quarterly, 1st ser., XX (1912), 261-262.
        [Corrected total £619,796.  The total in printed
        record appears to be £5,000 short.]

TABLE XIV: AMOUNT OF CASH ON HAND AND ACCOUNTS RECEIVABLE
AT END OF ACCOUNTING YEAR, WILLIAM PRENTIS &
COMPANY, 1734-1765; JOHN PRENTIS & COMPANY,
1767-1773; ROBERT PRENTIS & COMPANY, 1774-1775.

| Year | Cash on Hand £ Virginia Currency | Accounts Receivable £ Virginia Currency |
|------|----------------------------------|-----------------------------------------|
| 1734 | 631 | 3,184 |
| 1735 | 1,146 | 2,539 |
| 1736 | 345 | 2,622 |
| 1737 | 10 | 2,658 |
| 1738 | 85 | 2,717 |
| 1739 | 303 | 2,159 |
| 1740 | 330 | 2,499 |
| 1741 | 292 | 2,184 |
| 1742 | 346 | 2,205 |
| 1743 | 485 | 2,086 |
| 1745 | 855 | 2,944 |
| 1746 | 1,015 | 3,614 |
| 1748 | 204 | 4,253 |
| 1749 | 749 | 4,179 |
| 1750 | 515 | 4,558 |
| 1751 | 561 | 6,027 |
| 1753 | 469 | 8,303 |
| 1755 | 1,614 | 8,44[-] |
| 1757 | 1,034 | 8,575 |
| 1759 | 1,008 | 8,171 |
| 1761 | 1,306 | 8,728 |
| 1765 | 1,203 | 11,241 |
| 1767 | 70 | 12,238 |
| 1769 | 1,426 | 10,462 |
| 1771 | 1,258 | 10,638 |
| 1773 | 1,095 | 11,598 |
| 1774 | 1,044 | 11,926 |
| 1775 | 980 | 12,127 |

Source: Prentis Papers (University of Virginia).

the expiration of the term of credit.[60] William Reynolds of Yorktown requested long-term credit from a wholesale grocer in London in this way:

> I am in want of a few Articles in your way which [I] have Noted at foot...I make no doubt I shall be able to remitt you for them within the limited Credit of 12 Mo[nths]. but if I shou'd not [I] am willing to pay you Interest after 12 Months from the Shipping which I dont doubt you will think sufficient as it is a better Interest than you can make by your Money in the Stocks [i.e., British government bonds] & the loan of a few hundred pounds for two or three years wou'd be obliging me.[61]

The customary credit in the wholesale trade of West Indian and southern European commodities, extended by American importers to urban and backcountry retailers, was six to twelve months.[62] Probably, the term of payment was shorter in the case of small sales. A Yorktown storekeeper, who ordered one hogshead of rum from Neil Jamieson in 1774, spoke of six months as "the usual time of payment."[63] When

---

60. Ibid., p. 73.

61. William Reynolds to Richard Lawrence, December 23, 1773, Letterbook of William Reynolds, II.

62. Charles Steuart to Mr. Cardock, February 1, 1755; and to Scott, Pringle, Cheap & Company, June 25, 1763, Letterbook of Charles Steuart, II.

63. Thomas Lilly to Neil Jamieson, March 23, 1774, Papers of Neil Jamieson, XIX, pp. 4423-4424.

William Russell, a Williamsburg retailer, purchased three

hogsheads of rum from Jamieson in January, 1770, he promised

that "the Cash in April is Certain perhaps sooner as suits

me."[64] This would have involved a credit of four months or

less.

In spite of the importance of credit operations

to business, there was no credit-rating service to supply

financial data on prospective customers. The problems of

an English firm acquiring reliable information about the

credit standing of firms 3,000 miles away is obvious. Repu-

tations of the larger British houses were often better known

to colonial merchants than those of the smaller American

firms to the English.[65]

American merchants, of course, could determine

more readily the financial standing of enterprises in their

own cities.[66] However, in rapidly growing communities like

---

64. W. Russell to Neil Jamieson, January 17, 1770,
ibid., XI, p. 2433.

65. Foulke, Sinews of American Commerce, p. 74.

66. The Junto in Philadelphia, for example, provided
informal facilities for the communication of credit information on local business concerns. Two of the regular subjects discussed at the meetings were: "Hath any citizen in
your knowledge failed in business lately, and what have you
heard of the cause?" and "Have you lately heard of any
citizen's thriving well, and by what means?" Ibid., p. 66.

Norfolk, merchants often had difficulty checking the background of the many newcomers. This letter from a North
Carolina storekeeper warns of the too-ready acceptance of
a supposed fellow-countryman by the Scottish business community in Norfolk:

> Let me offer you a piece of Salutary advice: do
> not place so much Confidence in Strangers espe-
> cially Carolina men; though other Countrys are
> not without their Imposters, for I hear a Dutch-
> man named Kennedy now at Norfolk has found out
> the weak side of the People of that place, and
> passes amongst you for a Gent from Scotland, be-
> ware of him as he was formerly employed as Cashier
> to Some [Eng]lish Comp[an]y in the Austrian
> Netherlands & Elop[ed w]ith the Company's Cash.[67]

In the absence of facilities for gathering concrete
financial data, great importance was attached to reports of
a merchant's character and integrity. Reputation was a
zealously guarded business asset. When a West Indian correspondent accused Charles Steuart of not making a remittance
as promised, the latter replied:

> I scarce know any thing by which a Man in Trade
> would more Justly forfeit, not only his Credit
> as a Merchant, but, all right and tittle to the
> Character of an honest Man, than what you are
> pleas[ed] to accuse me of.[68]

---

67. Alexander Elmly to Neil Jamieson, March 18, 1764,
Papers of Neil Jamieson, III, p. 670.

68. Charles Steuart to Dr. Hone, August 14, 1754,
Letterbook of Charles Steuart.

A Virginian seeking a new connection in England usually secured a reference from a fellow-businessman in the colony. For example, William Reynolds of Yorktown wrote to a London merchant with whom he did regular business:

> Mr David Jameson of this Town desired me to write
> you to send him by first opportunity 5 C[w]t best
> single [refined] Sugar, he is a Man of fortune
> and one whom you may depend on he imports pretty
> largely and has told me he will write for all his
> Grocery from you & remitt you a bill for the Amount
> annually.[69]

The American importer seeking goods on credit might also refer the exporter to other British businessmen for information, as did Mary Rathell when she opened her millinery store in Williamsburg in 1772:

> perhaps Sir you May Scruple Sending so Much Goods
> to a person Who you know so little off, but you
> may depend on My being very Exact in My payments,
> and for a further Satisfaction to your self, I re-
> fer you for Particulars to your friend Coll. Geo.
> Mercer in Hollis Street, who is Not unaquainted
> with My Method of Dailing,....[70]

Similarly, backcountry retailers desiring credit from American importers offered references. A Leeds storekeeper wrote to Neil Jamieson of Norfolk: "As I am a stranger

---

69. William Reynolds to Richard Lawrence, June 8, 1774, Letterbook of William Reynolds, II.

70. Mary Rathell to John Norton, January 31, 1772, Mason, John Norton & Sons, pp. 217-218.

to you I referr yo[u]. to any of ye. tradeing Gent[lemen]. up
Rappa[hannock]. River."[71]

A firm approached for credit by someone unknown
or unrecommended to it usually made inquiries regarding the
prospective customer's local standing and reputation. The
investigation had to be made quietly, so that suspicion
might not be aroused. William Holt, who operated a flour
mill near Williamsburg, asked a Boston merchant to obtain
information about a man to whom he had sold some flour:

> Pray make y[ou]r. inquiry w[i]th. such Causion
> as may not effect his Credit, as I hope his in-
> tentions are hones, & it may be of Consequence
> to him to appear in a Creditable light at a
> place where I believe he is gone to settle a
> Correspondence.[72]

Since the credit investigation might take several
months, the British merchant was often tempted to make the
shipment immediately, before replies were received, so as
not to lose a sale.[73] Sometimes, security was required before the goods were delivered to a customer who was not

---

71.  Max Robinson to Neil Jamieson, July 15, 1765,
Papers of Neil Jamieson, V, p. 1119.

72.  William Holt to William Palfrey, May 29, 1772,
Palfrey Papers.

73.  Williamson, "Credit Relations Between Colonial and
English Merchants," pp. 58-60.

known to the shipper, although the colonial merchant might
resent this practice as much as the delay of a shipment to
await information on his credit standing. When a Bristol
firm directed its captain not to deliver an order of goods
to William Reynolds without security, the latter was quite
indignant. Reynolds immediately wrote that he "did not
expect...to have had them [i.e., the goods] shipt under
that disagreeable restriction," which he said was "a thing
quite new to me," and that he was "sorry that a Correspondence has commenc'd which must so shortly end."[74]

Since unsecured book credit was the usual form
in use, a demand for security of any kind for normal business debt was regarded as a reflection upon one's credit
standing. Thus, Harry Piper of Alexandria was understand-
ably surprised by a British exporter's proposal for landed
security for goods sold on credit to a storekeeper, as he
reported most of the information usually desired by the
English merchant:

> I observe what you say with regard to J M, I be-
> fore mentioned that it is very disagreeable to
> propose taking Mortgages from a Man in Trade, these
> things must be made publick --- his Credit has
> never yet been called in question, & it might

---

74. William Reynolds to Farell & Jones, July 12, 1774,
Letterbook of William Reynolds, I.

hurt him much --- I suppose if he was to Die, you
might lay out of your Money for some time, & that
might be the case with the best Man in the Country
--- His Brother is in the Store, who is a very
discreet Lad, & imagine will have the management
in case of any Accident. I can't find that he
owes many debts, & he has pretty considerable
property in Town, he has lately made a purchase
of Sebastians Houses & Lots, which is a very convenient place for a Store --- I am certain such
a proposal would shock him, & am yet to believe
which he would not agree to, as I dare say never
such a one was ever made to him ---[75]

Undoubtedly, some British exporters at times did
not check carefully the credit standing of Virginia merchants, particularly during periods of expansion. However,
it is unlikely that "the prevailing Mode of Trade" was
based on giving "extensive Credit" to many people of little
or no standing "who call themselves Merch[an]ts," as a
planter charged in 1773.[76]

In the country stores, the manager was charged
with the responsibility of knowing the debt-paying habits
and extent of property ownership of each of his customers.
Storekeepers were instructed on credit policy in this way:
"No man unless he has a Clear and Visible Estate must be

---

75. Harry Piper to Isaac Littledale, October 26, 1768,
Letterbook of Harry Piper (University of Virginia).

76. Robert Beverly to Samuel Athawes, February, 1773,
Letterbook of Robert Beverly (Library of Congress).

Credited with more than the Value of their Annuall Crops;
Observe to give no Creditt to Tradesmen or Overseers Unless
their Employers become Security for what they deal ---."[77]

When in spite of efforts to deal only with good
risks, the creditor found that the colonial debtor could
not pay, he was faced with the alternatives of likely loss
of much of the debt and of the customer's future patronage
as well, or continuing to give credit to help him to recover.
In many cases, the creditor decided that the latter policy
was wiser in the long run.[78] The debt, though, was usually
refunded by execution of a bond secured by collateral such
as real estate and by signatures of responsible guarantors.
In this case, the debt bore interest from the date of re-
funding. Bonding was preferable to instituting a suit in
court, although legal action still had to be taken if the
debtor defaulted on the bond.[79]

In the store trade, where planters' accounts were
supposed to be settled once a year, Robinson advised the

---

77. James Robinson to Robert Paton, February 8, 1773,
Letterbook of William Cuninghame & Company (National Library of Scotland), I.

78. Williamson, "Credit Relations Between Colonial
and English Merchants," p. 83.

79. Ibid., pp. 295-296.

Cuninghame storekeepers that:

> It often happens when a planter is largely in debt
> at settlement or when any Considerable sum of money
> is advanced them they will Offer a security on their
> Estate which should at all times be accepted even
> from those in the best Creditt....in this Country
> when Merchants is kept out of his money he reckons
> the getting of Interest paid a small compensation
> for the want of it.[80]

The procedure of bonding the debt of a James

River storekeeper who owed money to a Boston merchant was

typical:

> I have rec'[eive]d a power of Attorny from Mr.
> Coffin [the Boston creditor] with positive
> orders to get your Bond w[i]th good Security
> for whatever I think may be due to him after the
> Sale of the Corn you are to Ship him,...I give
> you this timely Notice, that you may come to
> Williamsb[ur]g properly prepar[e]d for that pur-
> pose...you may depend upon it [that] no one shall
> know anything of the Matter from me, as soon as the
> Vessell gets to James Town I shall go to
> W[illia]msb[ur]g. and there wait your coming...I
> hope for your own Credit Sake you will make no de-
> lay, that I may not be put to the very disagree-
> able Necessity of Employing an Attorney in the
> Affair,...[81]

The bond was negotiable and could be discounted

with merchants or others who had money to lend.  Thus,

---

80.  James Robinson to William Cuninghame, October 8,
1771, Letterbook of William Cuninghame & Company, I.

81.  William Palfrey to John Cocke, March 21, 1764,
Palfrey Papers.  Palfrey was a Boston merchant who made
regular voyages to Virginia in the 1760's.

Carter Braxton hoped in 1765 to use a bonded debt as capital to finance a business deal:

> I want to raise a Sum of Money to compleat some
> Purchases I have lately made & I believe it is
> in your Power to assist me in doing it, my Scheme
> is this, I have a Bond of Mr Browns payable in
> Dec[embe]r 1766 for one thousand Pounds St[e]r[lin]g
> with good Security, the Money to be paid in good
> Bills of Exchange or gold & silver. If I could
> dispose of this at a tolerable rate I could then
> do what I wanted. I presume there are Men in
> your Town who would lay out Money in this Way
> if they could expect to make any thing, I sup-
> pose if I sell it must be to a disadvantage and
> I would submit to a small one rather than not
> have the Money in Octo[be]r or Dec[embe]r Court.
> I shall esteem it a Fav[o]r if you will consult
> such People on this Matter as you may suppose
> would lay out Money in that way & acquaint me of
> their offers.[82]

Some British firms employed professional debt collectors, particularly in the 1760's and '70's. Under this procedure, a collector purchased the debts due to a firm or store at a substantial discount and received title to all of the claims.[83]

As a last resort, creditors turned to court action to collect debts. For example, Charles Steuart reported

---

82. Carter Braxton to Neil Jamieson, September 2, 1765, Papers of Neil Jamieson, V, p. 1166.

83. Robert P. Thomson, "The Merchant in Virginia 1700-1775," (Unpublished Ph.D. dissertation, University of Wisconsin, 1955), pp. 278-279.

in 1755 to William Bowden, a London merchant, that "I intend up to Williamsburg, and believe the maney delays & trifling excuses I meet with will oblige me to order some suits for you which shall advise you of in time."[84]

After 1736 most debtors' suits were filed in the Hustings Court in Williamsburg. A law of that year permitted this court an optional jurisdiction in all debt cases arising within the colony.[35] The hustings court was under the influence of mercantile-minded townsmen who were generally friendly to creditors, in contrast to the situation in most county courts, which were dominated by agrarian debtors. Merchants found county courts very dilatory in processing suits, particularly in times of depression. In some cases, justices of the peace delayed proceedings by not attending the court sessions.[86] A Richmond merchant reported in 1773 that "the Patriotic Magestrates in Amherst County, have resolved not to sit to do business but twice

---

84. Charles Steuart to William Bowden, June 23, 1755, Letterbook of Charles Steuart, I.

85. Hening, Statutes, IV, 542.

86. Coulter, "Virginia Merchant," pp. 237 ff. The principal exception in the county court system, as Coulter points out, was York County, whose court processed debt cases promptly and impartially, because of the influence exerted in the county by the mercantile Nelson family.

in the year, untill the Inhabitants are clear of debt."[87]
In contrast, an observer noted in 1770 that "Suits have
seldom remained undetermined longer than 3 or 4 Months" in
the Williamsburg Husting Court, "when they have remained
undetermined almost as many Years in most of the other
Courts."[88] When planters proposed in 1770 to limit the
hustings court's jurisdiction to cases of debt actually
arising within the city, one merchant commented that
"Debtors too often appear ready to take every Step in
their Power to delay the Payment of just Debts."[89]

When judgment was obtained in a debt case, the
creditor could prosecute writs of _fieri facias_ (to take
the debtor's personal property), _elegit_ (to take personal
and real property), or _capias ad satisfaciendum_ (to take
the body of the debtor).[90] If the creditor chose to seek
restitution from the debtor's property, the court directed

---

87. R. Donald to Charles Steuart, February 10, 1773,
Papers of Charles Steuart, MS. 5028, p. 29.

88. John Tazewell to John Norton, July 12, 1770, John
Norton & Sons Papers (Colonial Williamsburg).

89. _Ibid._

90. George L. Chumbley, _Colonial Justice in Virginia:
The Development of a Judicial System, Typical Laws and Cases
of the Period_ (Richmond: Dietz Press, 1938), p. 97.

the sheriff to hold a public sale. One merchant reported
this situation in 1766:

> when Judgments are obtained, there is such a
> Scarcity of Cash that if the peoples goods
> were not sold on Credit they would not get
> half the value of them and in such cases the
> Law gives the Sherif liberty to sell on
> Credit,...91

Imprisonment of a debtor was costly to the creditor,
as Harry Piper of Alexandria told his Whitehaven principals
in 1767:

> I have ordered Suit ag[ains]t. McIntosh & he
> is taken, but is quite Insolvent, as soon as
> Judg[e]m[en]t. he will lay in Jail his 20 days,
> & therefore have ord[ere]d. if that should be
> the case, to have him turn[e]d. out, as I can't
> think of maintaining him there to throw more
> Money away.92

Probably, creditors ordered imprisonment of debtors only
when the latter attempted to flee, as in this case reported
by a Falmouth storekeeper in 1773:

> Inclosed you have an Executive against the Body
> of Rancis Martin for £11..19..2 1/2. & Costs
> of an Attachement Viz 15 Shill[ing]s & 173 lb
> Tobacco at 1 1/2 d per pound for a Debt due to
> Falmouth Store --- the said Francis Martine
> made a moonlight flitting or in other words he
> Run away & I am certainly informed is now in a

---

91. John Snelson to Cust & Innes, September 1, 1766,
Letterbook of John Snelson (Southern Historical Collection).

92. Harry Piper to Dixon & Littledale, July 23, 1767,
Letterbook of Harry Piper.

Small Vesal trading up & down James River. he is
a Well looking, very Lusty, Likely Man, about
Twenty Six years of Age & I am informed he is
Owner of the Vesal he sails in; he carryd away a
Negro felow of his Own & Sold him some where on
James River which enabled him to purchase his
Vesal --- you will no doubt make all the enquiry
you can [page torn] him so as to recover the
debt if practicable youll See a Blank in the
Exec[utio]n. left for the name of the County
where he may be apprehended...[93]

The fact that debtors with a few fixed assets

could move readily to escape payment probably had some ef-

fect upon the rate of bad debt losses.  However, storekeepers

like those in the Cuninghame stores took care not to extend

credit to those not likely to pay, as indicated previously.

But merchants often had difficulty locating debtors who

moved to North Carolina, where the courts were even more

hostile to creditors than were the rural county courts of

Virginia.[94]  Precise data on over-all bad debt losses in

Virginia are not available.  However, one factor described

prospects of non-payment of store debts in this way: "I am

generally acquainted with people and their circumstances

[which] makes the Risque of Debts but small; [so] that we

_____

93.  Arthur Morson to Neil Jamieson, July 11, 1773,
Papers of Neil Jamieson, XVIII, p. 4088.

94.  Thomson, "Merchant in Virginia," pp. 280-281.

have Sildom any bad debts."[95]  Experience would vary from
time to time according to general economic conditions, since
a sharp decline in the price level would create difficulty
for debtors to make payments on debts contracted at a higher
price level.  Also, some merchants and storekeepers were
better able than others to size up good credit risks and to
determine the proper time to expand and contract the volume
of credit outstanding.[96]

Significance of the Credit System.  Much has been
written about the oppressive effects of credit upon the
Virginia planters.  Thomas Jefferson maintained that "the
planters were a specie of property annexed to certain mercantile houses in London."  His account of hereditary debts
passed "from father to son for many generations"[97] has been

---

95.  William Johnston to Neill Buchanan, October 4,
1739, Letterbook of Francis Jerdone, I.

96.  For example, data available on late eighteenth-
century Philadelphia show that one enterprise suffered in
bad debt losses only 1.4 per cent of total credit sales,
while another had a record of 38 per cent lost in unrecover-
able debts.  Three other enterprises had losses of 8.3,
10.2, and 12.5 per cent.  Plummer, "Consumer Credit in Colonial Philadelphia," pp. 397-398.

97.  Paul L. Ford, The Works of Thomas Jefferson (New
York: G. T. Putnam's Sons, 1904-1905), V, 28.

generally accepted, placing the use of credit instruments
in an unsavory light.

In actuality, Jefferson's generalizations apply
particularly to a relatively small group of large planters
in the colony, some of whom owed as much as £11,000 to
British merchants in 1775.[98] Accounting for this situation was a combination of extravagance and over-optimism
on the part of the planters, as well as threats by the
latter to withdraw their business unless extensions of
credit continued to be granted.[99]

In contrast to the Jeffersonian view of credit,
one scholar concluded, after studying scores of account
books of Virginia merchants, that the "average debt was
probably under £50 and was settled at the end of the year."[100]
Data from the American Loyalist Claims Commission papers
reveal more specifically the nature of the debt structure
in the years immediately prior to the American Revolution.

---

98. Isaac S. Harrell, Loyalism in Virginia: Chapters
in the Economic History of the Revolution (Durham: Duke
University Press, 1926), pp. 26-29.

99. Emory G. Evans, "Planter Indebtedness and the
Coming of the Revolution in Virginia," William and Mary
Quarterly, 3d ser., XIX (1962), 518-523.

100. Thomson, "Merchant in Virginia," pp. 282-283.

A careful analysis of the Virginia debts claimed by six merchants engaged in the consignment trade (five in London
and one in Bristol) shows that the average debt, among 162
claimed, amounted to £644 8 shillings sterling. Approxi-
mately one-half of the debts were for sums of less than
£100. Only twenty-nine of the 162 debtor accounts of these
six firms stood at £1,000 or more. An analysis of the
debtor accounts of two Glasgow firms whose factors purchased
tobacco and sold goods in the colony indicates an average
debt of £29 6 shillings, with 94 per cent of the 3,573
claimed debts below £100 sterling.[101]

That all planters were not "annexed to certain
mercantile houses" is evidenced by the fact that the names
of some debtors appeared among the claims of several merchants. Indeed, planters might prolong their credit by
deploying their remittances strategically among several
different consignment merchants and stores.[102] When a
planter did maintain fairly close relations with a specific
English firm over a long period of time, he often did so
because of loyalty inspired by personal friendship as well

---

101. Sheridan, "British Credit Crisis of 1772," pp. 179-
182.

102. Ibid., pp. 181, 185.

as the need to maintain a secure credit link.[103]

It should be emphasized, though, that credit was not obtained without cost to the user. Distribution of goods in a credit economy involved costs which, in the last analysis, had to be borne by the ultimate consumer. Thus, an interest charge for the use of credit was contained in the price. Robert Morris pointed out in 1786 that interest for the first year's credit in trade before the Revolution was "amply compensated by the advances put on the real cost of the goods."[104] The British exporter, since he received a discount for prompt payment to his suppliers,[105] usually offered the colonial merchant a discount of 5 per cent on whatever portion of the debt was paid before expiration of the term. However, it is not likely that American importers took extensive advantage of this opportunity to reduce costs.[1]

American importers, too, charged their customers

---

103.  Rosenblatt, "Significance of Credit in the Tobacco Consignment Trade," pp. 386-387.

104.  Quoted in Plummer, "Consumer Credit in Colonial Philadelphia," p. 395.

105.  Joshua Johnson to Wallace & Davidson, December 2, 1771, Letterbook of Wallace, Davidson & Johnson (Maryland Hall of Records.)

106.  Williamson, "Credit Relations Between Colonial and English Merchants," pp. 76-77.

a price which included the cost of credit, as this letter

to Neil Jamieson from a storekeeper on the James River in-

dicates:

> As our Concern is a new one and we cannot expect
> to be very flush of Money I shou'd hope that a
> payment in 12 Months might suit you for the first
> parcel of Goods, and I am afraid to promise a
> quicker [payment] --- Indeed I wou'd rather allow
> some difference in the price than be obliged to
> pay sooner, tho' I am hopeful you will be as
> moderate in this respect as you can.[107]

The method of calculating true interest charges

is shown also in this contract made in October, 1765, by

Jamieson and an iron producer:

> I acknowledge to have agreed with James Campbell
> for a Parcell of Pigg Iron at or about Thirty Tun's
> less or more, at the Price, and on the following
> Conditions viz. the whole vallue to be paid in
> Country Produce at the Curr[en]t. Price, and if
> Paid on or before the April Court, to Allow him
> at the Rate of five Pounds - fifteen shillings
> Virginia Curr[enc]y p[er] Tun Cont[a]ining Twenty
> two hundred & forty N[e]t. Pounds for each Tun,
> or if not Paid till after the April Court, in that
> Case to pay the vallue in Produce as above mentioned,
> at the Rate of Six Pounds Cur[renc]y p[er] Tun,...[108]

In other words, Jamieson received a discount of about 4 per

cent if he paid for the iron within six months.

---

107. Dan McCallum to Neil Jamieson, August 7, 1773,
Papers of Neil Jamieson, XVIII, p. 4133.

108. Contract of Neil Jamieson and James Campbell,
October 5, 1765, ibid., V, p. 1189.

There is some evidence to indicate the extent to which retailers charged different prices to cash and credit customers. Virginia stores usually sold merchandise at a goods price and at a cash price. The former, which was higher, was charged in cases where goods were purchased on credit. The lower cash price for merchandise was extended to customers not in debt to the store.[109] The policy in the Cuninghame stores in Virginia was generally to quote lower prices to the few who did pay cash for their goods, as well as to those who paid their accounts promptly. James Robinson, who supervised this chain of stores, felt that "it would be unjust as well as imprudent" to charge the same price to all, regardless of method of payment.[110]

Another kind of cost of credit to the community was periodic economic hardship occurring as the result of a breakdown of the system. So delicate was the balance of the credit mechanism, so interwoven were creditor-debtor relationships between Britain and Virginia and within the colony, that a breakdown at any one point had immense repercussions. A case in point was the experience of Virginians

---

109. Coulter, "Virginia Merchant," pp. 107-108.

110. James Robinson to William Cuninghame, October 8, 1771, Letterbook of William Cuninghame & Company, I.

during the British financial crisis of 1772-1773.

Briefly, the background of the crisis of 1772 and 1773 was this. The ultimate source of credit was London, the financial as well as the political capital of the British Empire. The English exporter, whether a consignment merchant or a supplier of retail stores, purchased his goods on credit from manufacturers or from other merchants, or he utilized the increasingly sophisticated financial mechanism being developed by London bankers during the eighteenth century.[111] Scotland suffered a shortage of capital, but the "Tobacco Lords" of Glasgow were able to raise money to finance their trade by drawing and redrawing bills of exchange on London agents. Under this system, a Scottish firm might draw a bill on its agent in London, payable in sixty days, before which time the latter would draw on his principal in Scotland for the same sum plus interest and commission. This device, usually repeated several times, was costly. More important, this structure of credit was subject to severe dislocations by any kind of shock. Thus, the absconding by the partner of a London

---

111. See T. S. Ashton, <u>An Economic History of England: The 18th Century</u> (New York: Barnes & Noble, Inc., 1954), Ch. VI, and D. M. Joslin, "London Private Bankers, 1720-1785," <u>Economic History Review</u>, 2d ser., VII (1954), 167-186

firm which handled this business for the Scottish bankers, Douglas, Heron and Company (the Ayr Bank), precipitated the crisis of 1772-1773.[112]

When merchants in England and Scotland felt the financial pinch resulting from this situation, they necessarily had to restrict the amount of credit outstanding in Virginia by limiting new grants of credit and by pressing for repayment of outstanding debts. The deflationary effect of this large-scale debt contraction was particularly burdensome to Virginians as it coincided with a decline in tobaccco prices.[113]

The breakdown of the credit mechanism created difficulties for merchants as well as for planters. For example, in May, 1773, Beverley Dickson, a Williamsburg storekeeper, wrote to John Norton, from whom he purchased the bulk of his merchandise: "My Collections have been very bad this Court which is the Reason of my Remitting you so small a sum But Sir you may rest assur'd that I shall

---

112. H. Hamilton, "The Failure of the Ayr Bank, 1772," Economic History Review, 2d ser., VIII (1956), 405-417. H. Hamilton, An Economic History of Scotland in the Eighteenth Century (Oxford: Clarendon Press, 1963), pp. 314-325. Sir John Clapham, The Bank of England: A History (New York: Macmillan, 1945), I, 242-247.

113. Sheridan, "British Credit Crisis of 1772," p. 184.

endeavour to make you punctual remittances."[114]

In spite of these problems raised by creditor-debtor relations, all parties concerned derived benefits. Merchants and storekeepers found that the only way to conduct business in an agricultural economy was to grant extensive amounts of credit. The high cost of credit in the colonial period, estimated later by Robert Morris to be "a rate of interest equal to 15, 20, or perhaps 30 per cent,"[115] must be regarded as a part of the social cost of the rapid economic development of a new country, where the price of capital, a factor of production in short supply, is usually high. More specifically, credit enabled the planter and the farmer "to divert to long-range projects cash and labor which otherwise would have had to be allocated to the needs of the hour: thus, he could speculate in land, buy slaves, and clear land for cultivation."[116]

---

114. Beverley Dickson to John Norton, May 10, 1773, Brock Collection (Huntington Library.)

115. Quoted in Plummer, "Consumer Credit in Colonial Philadelphia," p. 395.

116. Jacob M. Price, "The Rise of Glasgow in the Chesapeake Tobacco Trade 1707-1775," William and Mary Quarterly, 3d ser., XI (1954), 197. See also Rosenblatt, "Significance of Credit in the Tobacco Consignment Trade," pp. 398-399.

## C.   STERLING EXCHANGE

The Williamsburg Meeting of Merchants served as an informal clearinghouse for much of the business of Virginia. Many contracts for purchases of tobacco and other commodities stipulated that final settlement be made at the next Meeting.[117] Likewise, importers of foreign goods sought to make collections of debts due from storekeepers and individual customers.[118]

Most financial settlements involved foreign trade in one way or another. Thus the clearing of intra-Virginia credits was directly connected with the market for sterling exchange. It was necessary for tobacco buyers to make transfers of funds from their principals in Great Britain to pay for their cash purchases.[119] Although planters who consigned their tobacco to British merchants often ordered

---

117.   For example, Harry Piper pointed out that "the Merchants are generally engaged to make their Payments at the General Court." Piper to Dixon & Littledale, October 12, 1772, Letterbook of Harry Piper.

118.   See n. 114 above.

119.   When buyers purchased tobacco, they usually granted book credits against which sellers could draw to pay for goods. Often, though, some cash was necessary to attract sellers to the store. The proportion of cash varied with the position of the planter and the competitive situation in the area.

goods in payment, some chose to transfer at least a part of the proceeds of the sale of their produce.[120] On the other hand, Virginia importers of British goods had to transfer funds from the colony to make final payment in Britain. Specie and commodities were frequently used to settle foreign balances, but bills of exchange constituted the principal means of transferring funds between the colony and Britain.[121]

The Bill of Exchange. In a simplified exchange transaction, four persons were involved - two at the place where the bill was drawn and two at the place of payment. In Virginia, the drawer, a person with a claim on money in Britain - a tobacco factor or consignor - sold sterling credits to an importer of British goods for a sum in Virginia currency. The Virginia importer, the remitter, sent

---

120. Lewis C. Gray maintains that by the eve of the American Revolution most of the tobacco shipped on consignment was paid for by drawing bills of exchange on the consignee, rather than by ordering goods as had been the case in an earlier period. History of Agriculture in the Southern United States to 1860 (New York: Peter Smith, 1941), I, 426.

121. Cf. Arthur H. Cole, "Evolution of the Foreign-Exchange Market of the United States," Journal of Economic and Business History, I, (1929), 386, 389.

the bill to his British creditor, who became the possessor
and presented it to the drawee, the person on whom the bill
was drawn, for payment in sterling.[122]

The bill of exchange was negotiable when it was
endorsed by the persons to whose order it had been drawn.
Bills could be endorsed as many times as desired, but each
endorser was liable for the face amount in case of non-payment.[123]

Bills could be drawn payable at sight - that is,
payable on the date on which they were presented to the
drawee for acceptance - or for a term of days or months
after sight. Acceptance, denoted by the drawee's signature
on the bill, indicated that he would pay the specified sum
at the required time. Usance, a term sometimes used on the
bill, meant the customary length of time that a bill had to
run between acceptance and payment. Usance varied between
different points of trade, but it was generally fixed at
sixty days after sight in the trade between Britain and

---

122. John Mair, Book-keeping Methodiz'd: or a Methodical Treatise of Merchant-Accompts, 2nd ed. (Edinburgh:
W. Sands, 1741), p. 196.

123. Ibid., p. 198.

Virginia.[124]

To insure against loss in transit, four copies

of a bill were made by the drawer; the first copy to be

presented for payment cancelled the three other copies.

The drawer was required to inform the drawee by letter of

the sum drawn, time of payment, and other circumstances of

the bill, "to prevent forgeries and that he who is drawn upon

may not be surprised with the Draught."[125]

Protesting meant refusal to make payment on the

bill. A bill was protested usually for one of two reasons:

(1) non-acceptance, the refusal of the drawee to accept the

bill for payment due to lack of funds in the drawer's ac-

count; or (2) non-payment, the inability of the drawee to

make payment at the specified time because of his own lack

of funds.[126] Damages on protested bills, levied against

---

124. Ibid., p. 199. Usance on bills from London to
France, for example, was thirty days; from London to Spain
and Portugal, two months; and from London to Genoa and
other cities in Italy, three months. There was some difference among the different colonies in regard to usance.
In Philadelphia, for example, bills on London were customarily drawn at forty days sight. Anne Bezanson, Robert
D. Gray, and Miriam Hussey, Prices in Colonial Pennsylvania (Philadelphia: University of Pennsylvania Press, 1935),
p. 320.

125. Mair, Book-keeping Methodiz'd, p. 197.

126. Ibid., pp. 201-202. Mair notes a third reason

the drawer, usually amounted to 10 to 20 per cent of the face value of the bill, plus interest charges from the date of protest.[127]

Because protested bills often resulted in business losses greater than the amount of damages and interest, purchasers of bills directed special attention to the financial standing of the drawer and drawee. Virginia law required "the drawers and indorsers of protested bills to repay the like sum of Current money that was paid for the bills," but a rise in exchange rates might "sweep away the whole damage of bills."[128] Bills drawn or endorsed by men of good reputation usually commanded a premium; those drawn by men with a previous record of protested bills were purchased with reluctance. Sometimes, endorsing of a bill was required in the case of a drawer not well known, for which service a fee of 2 1/2 per cent was levied.[129]

---

for protesting, "for better security," in cases when "there is good Reason to fear that he [i.e., the drawee] may turn insolvent before the Time of Payment."

127. Williamson, "Credit Relations Between Colonial and English Merchants," p. 48, n. 53.

128. Charles Steuart to William Bowden, February 15, 1757, Letterbook of Charles Steuart, II.

129. Williamson, "Credit Relations Between Colonial and English Merchants," pp. 29, 51.

Sometimes, planters who consigned their tobacco to London drew upon their correspondents, before accounts of the net proceeds had been received, for sums considerably larger than their balances. If the planter's credit was believed to be good, the London merchant accepted the overdraft; in other cases, he refused to accept the bill and returned it to Virginia, marked protested. At times, the volume of protested Virginia bills was considerable. Charles Steuart remarked in 1754 that "a very little acquaintance with this Country would remove your Surprize that Gentlemen draw without Effects which is too frequent[ly] practiced here."[130] However, he advised correspondents that he would "be particularly carefull to purchase good Bills which a general Acquaintance in the Country gives us an opportunity of knowing."[131]

Since London was the financial center of the British Empire, bills payable in that city were most in demand. Bills drawn on other cities in Britain usually sold

---

130. Charles Steuart to Mr. Cheslyn, June 17, 1754, Letterbook of Charles Steuart, I.

131. Charles Steuart to John Maynard, May 13, 1752, ibid., I.

at a lower rate.[132] At times, it was difficult to negotiate
a bill payable in an outport. Harry Piper of Alexandria,
who purchased tobacco for a Whitehaven firm, commented in
November, 1768, that "only Bills Paya[ble]. in London would
be taken, which will be rather hard on the Out Ports."[133]
This situation recurred in May, 1770, as "none but Londo[n].
Bills would do at the Gen[era]l Court,"[134] and again in
August, 1771, when "it is now difficult passing Bills except they are Payable in London."[135] But Piper reported to
his principals in June, 1772, that he was "obliged for your
particular care of my Bills, they are in good Credit here,
or else I should be oftener Obliged to draw Pay[abl]e. in
Londo[n]."[136] In October, 1773, he noted that his bills
on Whitehaven were "in as good Credit as any out port Bills,

132. Williamson, "Credit Relations Between Colonial
and English Merchants," pp. 29-30.

133. Harry Piper to Dixon & Littledale, November 15,
1768, Letterbook of Harry Piper.

134. Harry Piper to Dixon & Littledale, May 28, 1770,
ibid.

135. Harry Piper to Dixon & Littledale, August 16,
1771, ibid.

136. Harry Piper to Dixon & Littledale, June 15, 1772,
ibid.

but London ones are still preferred."[137]

Organization of the Exchange Market. In economically decentralized Virginia, the Williamsburg Meeting of
Merchants provided the major market for sterling exchange.
Even where bills were bought and sold elsewhere in the colony, the Williamsburg quotations governed transactions.
For example, when Charles Steuart supplied cash to the
captain of a ship which arrived at Portsmouth in 1761, he
was careful to point out that he took the captain's bills
on the British shipowner at the rate determined at the last
previous Meeting.[138]

Unlike the highly organized exchange markets of
the present day, there were no exclusively specialized
dealers or bankers in foreign exchange. Rather, those with
credits in Great Britain drew bills of exchange against
these balances and sold their bills directly to others
seeking to make remittances abroad. In Williamsburg, the
buyers and sellers of sterling bills assembled at "the

---

137. Harry Piper to Dixon & Littledale, October 24,
1773, ibid.

138. Charles Steuart to Anthony Bacon & Company,
December 19, 1761, Letterbook of Charles Steuart, II.

Exchange", which was an open street back of the Capitol.[139]

Exchange stood at par, 25, when £125 in Virginia currency purchased £100 sterling. This difference between the two currencies was based on the value which Virginia assigned to silver, 6 shillings 8 pence per ounce, as compared to the sterling price of 5 shillings 2 pence.[140] The actual rate of exchange, however, fluctuated considerably, from below 15 to over 65. As contemporaries pointed out, the price of sterling in Virginia was "regulated chiefly by the Quantity of Money and the Number of Bills brought to Market."[141] At times when the supply of cash was "so scarce, that there was not sufficient at the General Court to satisfie the demand of the Drawers,"[142] the exchange rate declined. If "there was more money than Bills,"[143]

---

139. Governor Fauquier to the Lords of Trade, November 3, 1765. C.O. 5/1331, ff. 54-59, Public Record Office. (Photostat in Research Department, Colonial Williamsburg).

140. Ripley, Financial History of Virginia, pp. 132-133.

141. R. C. Nicholas to Virginia Gazette, July 16, 1773, in "Paper Money in Virginia," p. 235.

142. Harry Piper to Dixon & Littledale, November 25, 1768, Letterbook of Harry Piper.

143. James Robinson to William Cuninghame & Company, June 25, 1774, Letterbook of William Cuninghame & Company.

the price of sterling rose. Tables XV and XVI show the course of exchange in the eighteenth century.

Ultimately, the price of exchange varied with the balance of payments between Virginia and Britain. The supply of bills depended upon the quantity of tobacco and other commodities exported to Britain and upon their prices there. In addition, Virginia had an indirect source of supply of sterling credits secured through trade with the West Indies and southern Europe, since merchants usually transmitted to London at least a part of the proceeds of sales to those areas. The demand for bills rested upon the quantity and prices of goods imported from Great Britain. Another demand for sterling was represented by importations of slaves from Africa, which usually commanded specie or bills of exchange.

The exchange rate quoted at Williamsburg was generally for bills drawn on London, payable sixty days after presentation. Bills drawn for a longer period, or made payable at an outport, sold for a lower price.[144] Bills were usually drawn "at the instant the money is paid." However, money could be obtained at a General Court in April or

---

144. For example, in 1773 bills drawn on London sold at 32 1/2, those on outports at 30. Charles Yates to Samuel Martin, December 10, 1773, Letterbook of Charles Yates (University of Virginia).

October for a bill to be drawn at the following Court of Oyer and Terminer in June or December. For this accommodation of two months, the drawer received 2 1/2 per cent less than the current exchange rate.[145]

The sellers of bills - the purchasers of tobacco who needed cash to conclude deals and the consignors who received payment by drawing against balances in Britain - obviously desired a high exchange rate to increase the value of their sterling credits in terms of Virginia currency. For the tobacco buyer, a decline in the exchange rate resulted in an increase in the sterling cost of tobacco, since a larger amount in sterling bills would have to be drawn to cover the currency cost of tobacco purchased.[146] The growth of the grain trade and the current depression in tobacco led one observer to regard wheat purchasers as the most important drawers of bills in 1774.[147] They too

---

145. Francis Jerdone to Spiers & Brown, December 10, 1756, Letterbook of Francis Jerdone.

146. As Harry Piper pointed out when exchange reached a low level in 1770, "if this does not effect the price of Tobacco the Sterling price must be very high." Harry Piper to Dixon & Littledale, January 27, 1770, Letterbook of Harry Piper.

147. James Robinson to William Cuninghame & Company, May 28, 1774, Letterbook of William Cuninghame & Company.

TABLE  XV:  AVERAGE ANNUAL EXCHANGE RATES, VIRGINIA CUR-
RENCY ON STERLING, 1740-1775

| Year | Price of Sterling in Virginia Currency |
|------|----------------------------------------|
| 1740 | 22 1/2 |
| 1741 | 20 |
| 1742 | 20 |
| 1743 | 20 |
| 1744 | 20 |
| 1745 | 30 |
| 1746 | 33 1/2 |
| 1747 | 40 |
| 1748 | 33 1/2 |
| 1749 | 22 1/2 |
| 1750 | 27 1/2 |
| 1751 | 30 |
| 1752 | 30 |
| 1753 | 30 |
| 1754 | 27 1/2 |
| 1755 | 30 |
| 1756 | 35 |
| 1757 | 40 |
| 1758 | 37 1/2 |
| 1759 | 40 |
| 1760 | 40 |
| 1761 | 45 |
| 1762 | 60 |
| 1763 | 62 1/2 |
| 1764 | 60 |

TABLE XV: (cont'd)

| | |
|---|---|
| 1765 | 60 |
| 1766 | 25 |
| 1767 | 25 |
| 1768 | 25 |
| 1769 | 20 |
| 1770 | 19 1/2 |
| 1771 | 20 |
| 1772 | 25 |
| 1773 | 30 |
| 1774 | 30 |
| 1775 | 25 |

Source: Chart showing exchange rates averaged annually, prepared by John M. Hemphill, Colonial Williamsburg Research Department, for notations of exchange rates on protested bills, account books, letters, etc.

TABLE XVI:   THE COURSE OF EXCHANGE, 1764-1773

| | | | |
|---|---|---|---|
| 1764 | May | 60 | |
| | November | 60 | |
| 1765 | May | 65 | |
| | November | 55 | |
| | December | 40 | |
| 1766 | March | 22 1/2-25 | |
| | June | 25 | |
| | November | 25 | |
| | December | 27 1/2 | |
| 1767 | April | 27 1/2 | |
| | June | 30 | |
| | November | 25 | |
| | December | 25 | |
| 1768 | May | 25 | |
| | June | 27 1/2 | |
| | November | 25 | |
| 1769 | May | 22 1/2 | |
| | June | 22 1/2 | |
| | October | 20 | |
| | December | 15 | |
| 1770 | May | 15 | |
| | July | 17 1/2 | |
| | November | 20 | |
| | December | 17 1/2 | |
| 1771 | May | 20 | |
| | November | 20 | |
| | July | 20 | |
| | December | 20 | |
| 1772 | May | 20 | |
| | August | 25 | |
| | October | 25 | |
| | December | 25 | |
| 1773 | May | 30 | |

Source:   Memorandum compiled by Neil Jamieson [May, 1773]
Papers of Neil Jamieson, XVII, p. 4011.

sought a high rate of exchange.

Those who purchased bills, commonly termed the "moneyed men," were in large measure importers of British manufactured goods. There were importers in all of the towns of Virginia, but the most important single group consisted of the "Norfolk men" from the largest commercial center of the colony.[148] They generally worked for a low exchange rate, since they could then pay their sterling debts with a smaller amount of Virginia currency.

Government officials also entered the exchange market, since they had to make regular remittances to England. Like other purchasers of bills, Receiver-General Corbin desired a low price for sterling exchange, as he complained in 1766 of "the great loss, Occasioned by the high Exchange, to his Majesty's Revenue" from the quitrents.[149]

---

148. For example, Francis Jerdone, a tobacco buyer, related how "the Norfolk men have combin'd together to effect" a "fall [in] the Exchange" in 1759. Francis Jerdone to Spiers & Brown, April 28, 1759, Letterbook of Francis Jerdone, II.

149. Richard Corbin to John Roberts, February 8, 1766, Letterbook of Richard Corbin (Colonial Williamsburg). Corbin remitted between £4,700 and £3,400 annually from 1762-1766, almost all in bills of exchange. Capel & Osgood in Account Current with Richard Corbin as Receiver General, Corbin Papers (Colonial Williamsburg).

Robert Carter Nicholas, treasurer of the provincial government, likewise remitted funds to Britain to discharge the
obligations of the Virginia government, such as the payment
of the salary of the colony's agent in London.[150]

According to the rules adopted in Williamsburg
in 1769, the rate of exchange was to be determined during
the first three days of the Meeting. Often, though, a
longer period was needed to settle the struggle between
drawers and remitters. One tobacco buyer described the
session of June, 1770, in this way: "The last Oyer Court
may be Calld a Remarkable one...from the time we pass'd before the Business of Exchange was settled. We were no less
than fourteen days. During the last eight days there was
a hard Struggle to fix the Rate of Exchange. The principall
drawers stood Out for 20 per Cent and the moneyd men Offerd
only 15 of which they were the most tenacious...However on
Saturday the last of June we brought it to a Compromise
and Received 17 1/2 per Cent [for] Bills Chiefly drawn on

---

150. Nicholas remitted sums as large as £1,365 in January, 1769; £2,439 in November, 1769; and £2,443 in May,
1771. Robert C. Nicholas to John Norton, January 13, 1769,
November 4, 1769, May 16, 1771, Mason, John Norton & Sons,
pp. 83, 109, 157. John Norton & Sons of London handled
the account of the Virginia Treasury as well as the personal
business of Nicholas.

London."[151]

Outright manipulation of the exchange market was sometimes proposed. William Allason reported in 1766 that a Scottish merchant, financed by a Glasgow bank to the extent of £150,000-200,000, had devised a plan to purchase all of the currency in Virginia with bills at a high exchange; he intended then to bring exchange down by withdrawing the money from circulation and to sell the currency at a lowered exchange to make a profit of £20,000. However, the exchange rate fell before the scheme could be undertaken.[152] In another instance, in 1772, a tobacco purchaser suggested that one or two factors might dispose of all of the bills drawn on the Glasgow companies. By reducing the competition among sellers, "the holder of a Bill...may be able to command his own price."[153] However, the major obstacle to the success of such a scheme was that drawers in immediate need of cash usually had to sell their bills at whatever might be the current rate of exchange.

---

151. James Robinson to David Walker, July, 1770, Letterbook of William Cuninghame & Company, I.

152. Edith E. B. Thomson, "A Scottish Merchant in Falmouth in the Eighteenth Century," Virginia Magazine of History and Biography, XXXIX (1931), 230.

153. James Robinson to William Cuninghame & Company, June 1, 1772, Letterbook of William Cuninghame & Company, II.

Some stabilization of the price of sterling at Williamsburg was achieved through intercolonial exchange transactions. When exchange rates were lower in Virginia than in other colonies, holders of sterling credits sold bills of exchange on London in the Philadelphia market and imported the specie. Because James Robinson expected the exchange rate to be below par at the meeting of October, 1771, he shipped £4,000 sterling in bills, drawn on the Cuninghame firm, to Willing and Morris of Philadelphia with orders to negotiate if exchange there stood at par or above.[154] In 1770, drawers of bills proposed "going even as far as Boston in quest of Cash."[155]

However, there were times when specie could not be obtained from other colonies to halt the drop in the exchange rate at Williamsburg. One observer reported in May, 1769, that "Sundry of the Factors for the great Companies have been at Philadelphia & New York after Specie & returned

---

154. James Robinson to Andrew Chalmer, September 28, 1771, Letterbook of William Cuninghame & Company, I. If the transaction was made as planned, Robinson directed Willing & Morris to ship the "hard Dollars", to be used by the Cuninghame storekeepers, "to the Care of Messrs. Neil Jamieson & Co." and to advise Mr. James Glassford of that firm so that "they may be taken proper care Off." - Robinson to William Henderson, October 8, 1771, ibid., I.

155. William Aitchison to Charles Steuart, March 15, 1770, Charles Steuart Papers, MS. 5040, p. 91.

with but a part of the Sum they intended to procure."[156]

A few months earlier, an Alexandria factor had lamented

that the Exchange "must fall" due to the scarcity of cash,

and that "the recourse we used to have to the Northward is

also stopped, for Gold & Silv[e]r. is not to be got there."[157]

In this kind of situation, when exchange was under

par in most of the colonies, the importation of specie from

Great Britain was urged to bolster the price of sterling in

Virginia.[158]  John Snelson wrote to his English correspon-

dent in 1770 that a Portuguese coin valued at 36 shillings

in sterling "will go here for about 46 shillings so that you

may know whether you can with Insurance and Interest for

lying out of your Money make it answer."[159]  However, the

shortage of currency in Britain itself and the profitable

---

156.  William Allason to Robert Allason & John Gray,
May 2, 1769, Letterbook of William Allason.

157.  Harry Piper to Dixon & Littledale, January 7,
1769, Letterbook of Harry Piper.

158.  William Aitchison of Norfolk wrote in 1770 that
"unless the Merch[an]ts. at Home supply their factors
w[i]t[h]. Specie, it [i.e., the exchange rate] will fall
lower." Aitchison to Charles Steuart, January 2, 1770,
Charles Steuart Papers, MS. 5026, p. 1.

159.  John Snelson to Edward Harford, December 10, 1770,
Letterbook of John Snelson.

172

alternative uses for bullion, such as trade with India and
the Far East,[160] tended to discourage shipments of specie
to America.

One way for tobacco buyers to avoid the disturbing
effect of declining exchange rates was to agree with tobacco
sellers at a sterling price. Roger Atkinson reported to
his principals in 1770 that he was hedging against an expected low rate of exchange by negotiating his contracts in
this way.[161] As Harry Piper pointed out in 1773, "it makes
no odd when I owe a Sterling debt [for a purchase of to-
bacco] whether I fix the Exchange at 20 or 24 per Cent or
any other Exchange."[162] On other occasions, purchasers of
export commodities might postpone drawing, at least tempo-
rarily, if they believed that exchange rates would rise.
Jerdone wrote to his principals in 1759: "My drafts on you
would have been for a much larger sum at this time, if I
could have got 35 per Cent for all I stand in immediate

---

160.  See Ashton, Economic History of England: The 18th
Century, Ch. V and VI, and A. E. Feavearyear, The Pound
Sterling: A History of English Money (Oxford: Clarendon
Press, 1931), Chapter VII.

161.  Roger Atkinson to Lyonel & Samuel Lyde, April 28,
1770, Letterbook of Roger Atkinson (University of Virginia).

162.  Harry Piper to Dixon & Littledale, April 12, 1773,
Letterbook of Harry Piper.

need of, but I am determin'd to suffer many inconveniences rather than fall the Exchange to 32 1/2 per Cent."[163] How-ever, when it was necessary to make final settlement of con-tracts, most tobacco buyers could not defer selling bills.

In the event of a higher exchange rate in Virginia than in other colonies, bills flowed to the Williamsburg market. Thus, one drawer in 1771 noted the possibility of a drop in the price of sterling "Occasion'd by...the lowness of the exchange to the Northward, from which Quarter many [bills] have been pour'd in upon us."[164] When remitters in Virginia found that the price of sterling was lower in Philadelphia than in Williamsburg, they shipped specie to Pennsylvania to buy exchange.[165] In the summer of 1772, Virginia remitters attempted to reduce the rate at Williams-burg by sending a reported £8,000-10,000 of specie to the Philadelphia market. However, the drawers advised their correspondents in the latter city of this strategy of the "moneyed men." Thus, as one bill seller reported, "the

---

163. Francis Jerdone to Spiers & Brown, April 28, 1759, Letterbook of Francis Jerdone.

164. James Robinson to William Cuninghame & Company, November 29, 1772, Letterbook of William Cuninghame & Com-pany, II.

165. James Balfour to John Norton, November 5, 1769, Mason, John Norton & Sons, p. 110.

purchasers of Bills were obliged to come to our terms."[166]

There was the possibility of settling debts by shipping specie to Britain when exchange rate rose to a high level. One trader pointed out in 1773 that "at the April Court there were many that rather than give 30 per Cent remitted home their specie."[167] But the scarcity of gold and silver on many occasions limited the practice of making bullion shipments to avoid payment of a high price for sterling exchange. Another difficulty was the high cost of shipping bullion during war time, so that exchange rates might rise to fairly high levels before remitters found it profitable to ship specie rather than to purchase bills.[168]

A remitter might dodge high exchange rates by postponing the purchase of bills, if his credit standing in Britain was sufficiently good. For example, William Reynolds of Yorktown explained to his London creditor in

---

166. James Robinson to William Cuninghame & Company, August 5, 1772, Letterbook of William Cuninghame & Company, II.

167. Harry Piper to Dixon & Littledale, October 24, 1773, Letterbook of Harry Piper.

168. Charles Steuart to George Keith, September 16, 1751, Letterbook of Charles Steuart. Steuart reported: "We shall remit the money in the best Manner we can,...

the summer of 1772 that he had intended "remitting some
Bills from this last meeting but our Exchange being raised
5 per Cent [I] shall defer it till October...at which time
it is generally thought that they will again be 20 per
Cent."[169]  In some cases, remitters preferred investing in
short-term loans in Virginia to purchasing bills of exchange
at a high price.  Francis Jerdone wrote to a British exporter
in 1762 that whatever of the latter's funds he collected
"Mr. Holt is willing to take on interest as you rather choose
to have it in his hands, than remitted at the present high
exchange."[170]

Thus, buyers and sellers of bills had to assess
many influences affecting the demand for and the supply of
exchange before determining the true price of sterling.
The Meetings in Williamsburg brought together the possessors
of sterling credits and the holders of currency from the
widely scattered commercial centers of Virginia.  Even though

---

but imagin it cannot be done in any Specie that can now be
got, under 30 P[er] C[en]t. for Dollars & Portugal Gold
are almost all Ship'd and but few Pistoles passing."  See
also Bezanson et al, Prices in Colonial Pennsylvania, p. 317.

169.  William Reynolds to John Norton, August 10, 1772,
Letterbook of William Reynolds.

170.  Francis Jerdone to Capt. Archibald Crawford,
October 14, 1762, Letterbook of Francis Jerdone.

it was still necessary for merchants to travel to county courts to make many of their collections and payments,[171] the periodic gathering provided facilities for the settlement of debts contracted in all parts of the colony. In these ways, the Williamsburg Meeting of Merchants performed many of the functions necessary to the financing of the business of the Old Dominion, although it lacked the formal organization and specialized facilities of a modern money market, or even those of London in the eighteenth century.

---

171. For example, Jerdone sold bills of exchange at the April, 1757, Meeting and used the proceeds to redeem promissory notes which were payable at the May Court of Hanover Court to make a final settlement for a purchase of tobacco. Francis Jerdone to Spiers & Brown, February 10, 1757, Letterbook of Francis Jerdone.

IV


PROBLEMS OF THE MEETING OF MERCHANTS


The periodic Meeting of Merchants at Williamsburg provided the businessmen of economically decentralized Virginia an opportunity to conduct many types of business. Despite the lack of formal organization before 1769, merchants travelled regularly to the capital or appointed a fellow-trader to represent them.[1] Definite rules to facilitate trading were adopted in 1769. Yet Meetings in the 1770's were frequently so late in starting or were so poorly attended that merchants found it difficult to transact their affairs in Williamsburg.

From the Meeting scheduled for October 25, 1770, one merchant wrote on November 5 that "No Business is yet done here."[2] In the following spring, Neil Jamieson stated

---

1. For example, William Carr of Dumfries usually sold bills of exchange for Harry Piper of Alexandria at the Meetings. Harry Piper to Dixon & Littledale, May 12, 1770, Letterbook of Harry Piper (University of Virginia).

2. Roger Atkinson to John Ponsonby, November 5, 1770, Letterbook of Roger Atkinson (University of Virginia).

that "the people up the County will not be in here before the 3d. or 4th." of May for the April 25 session,[3] but Atkinson complained that little business was being transacted on May 6.[4]

A similar situation prevailed in the following year. James Robinson reported on May 7, almost two weeks after the scheduled start of the April Meeting: "The Merchants from different parts of the Colony are not all come to Town and altho it is so late there is no business done."[5] This Meeting was so late in finishing its tasks that merchants agreed to postpone until July 20 the session regularly scheduled for June.[6] However, Atkinson wrote from Williamsburg on July 21: "The Merch[an]ts, altho' it is a Month later than common, are not yet met at this place."[7] Robinson

---

3. Neil Jamieson to James Glassford, April 26, 1771, Papers of Neil Jamieson (Library of Congress), XIII, p. 2968.

4. Roger Atkinson to Lyonel & Samuel Lyde, May 6, 1771, Letterbook of Roger Atkinson.

5. James Robinson to William Cuninghame & Company, May 7, 1772, Letterbook of William Cuninghame & Company (National Library of Scotland), II.

6. Virginia Gazette (Purdie & Dixon), May 21, 1772.

7. Roger Atkinson to "Brother," July 21, 1772, Letterbook of Roger Atkinson.

reported that the exchange rate was not settled at this Meeting until August 4.[8]

Since the April and October Meetings, coinciding with the General Court sessions, often terminated their business so late, it was formally agreed in November, 1772, to assemble in January and July rather than during the Oyer Court in December and June.[9] Neither this change in time nor the threat of fines to be levied on those who failed to come to the sessions resulted in prompt attendance of all members of the business community. Neil Jamieson, who had gone to Williamsburg for the Meeting scheduled to start on January 25, 1773, wrote on February 1 that "as yet no business is done, nor do I know what will be done, nor when I shall get home."[10]

James Glassford, who represented the Jamieson firm at the July Meeting, reported on August 3 that:

---

8. James Robinson to William Cuninghame & Company, August 5, 1772, Letterbook of William Cuninghame & Company, II.

9. Virginia Gazette (Purdie & Dixon), November 26, 1772. This agreement provided that those engaged in business in the colony "give their Attendance...in Person, or by their Representatives, on the twenty fifth Days of January, April, July, and October."

10. Neil Jamieson to James Glassford, February 1, 1773, Papers of Neil Jamieson, XVII, p. 3802.

> Of All the Courts or meetings you was ever at
> in this place I am persuaded you never was at such
> a one as this I do not find that the least sort of
> business of any kind has yet been done The
> Gent[leme]n from Peter[s]b[ur]g and some from
> James River are not yet come to Town when they
> will come is uncertain and when the business will
> be begun to afterward is more so.[11]

Four days later, Thomas Nelson, Jr., wrote that the "Mer-

chants of this Country are not yet collected together to

transact business."[12]  After two weeks, the few who came to

Williamsburg returned home without determining the exchange

rate.[13]

Neil Jamieson went to Williamsburg for the October,

1773, Meeting, heard that "the James River Gent[lemen]. will

not be down till the 8th." of November, and decided to go

to Richmond to attend to business there.[14]  A month later,

Jamieson wrote from Williamsburg that "its yet Uncertain

what time I shall be ready to leave this place, there is

---

11.  James Glassford to Neil Jamieson, August 3, 1773,
Papers of Neil Jamieson, XVIII, pp. 4130-4131.

12.  Thomas Nelson, Jr., to John Norton & Son, August 7,
1773, Letterbook of William and Thomas Nelson (Virginia
State Library Archives).

13.  Robert P. Thomson, "The Merchant in Virginia, 1700-
1775" (Unpublished Ph.D. dissertation, University of Wisconsin, 1955), p. 297.

14.  Neil Jamieson to James Glassford, October 27, 1773,
Papers of Neil Jamieson, XVIII, p. 4247.

not yet any appearances of business."[15]

       James Robinson summarized well the problem created by the lack of prompt attendance to transact business. As he was about to depart from Falmouth at the end of May in 1774 to attend the April Meeting, Robinson explained to his employers:

> This meeting has been long postponed, indeed we
> have been for years past detained so long in Town
> before the whole company were assembled that every
> person is in doubt when to go: As he is loth to be
> there before the bulk to lose so much time - At-
> tempts have been made and resolutions signd by
> numbers of the Trade to meet at a certain day
> during the sitting of the Generall Court, but they
> have here very small effect, soon become obsolett
> and greatly discourages any further tryall.[16]

"The time appointed for the Meeting of the Merch[an]ts in Williamsburg have been so badly observed of late," wrote Robert Pleasants, "that I apprehend they must fall on some other method in future by which to regulate the fulfilling [of] their contracts."[17]

       So serious was the difficulty in making transactions

---

15.  Neil Jamieson to Neil Jamieson & Company, November 28, 1773, ibid., XIX, pp. 4290-4291.

16.  James Robinson to William Cuninghame & Company, May 28, 1774, Letterbook of William Cuninghame & Company, II.

17.  Robert Pleasants to "Dear Friend," February 19, 1774, Letterbook of Robert Pleasants (College of William and Mary).

that seventy-two merchants found it necessary to state in June, 1774, that they had "resolved and are determined, for the future, to meet" in Williamsburg, "every 25th day of October and April; of which we give this publick Notice, that those who have Business to transact with us may know when to attend."[18]

In large part, the difficulties in enforcing attendance at the Meetings resulted from the impact of depression after 1772. Since the Meeting was the clearing-house for credits in the colony, it is not surprising that "those who owe & cannot pay must keep out of Williamsburg."[19] Also controversy over the proper policy of Virginians toward the revenue and regulatory measures of the British government very likely contributed to the difficulties of doing business at the Meetings. Merchants and planters had generally cooperated against the Stamp Act in 1765 and 1766, as London and Glasgow firms took a strong position in opposing the measure.[20] But merchants only reluctantly followed the

---

18. Virginia Gazette (Purdie & Dixon), June 30, 1774.

19. Charles Yates to Samuel Martin, December 10, 1773, Letterbook of Charles Yates (University of Virginia). See Richard B. Sheridan, "The British Credit Crisis of 1772 and the American Colonies," Journal of Economic History, XX (1960), 161-186.

20. Edith B. Thomson, "A Scottish Merchant in Falmouth

leadership of planters in establishing a boycott of British
goods after the Townshend Act. A non-importation agreement
was concluded at the Meeting of June, 1770, but the movement
was abandoned a year later.[21] And by the spring of 1774,
the train of events touched off by news of the passage of
the Coercive Acts was in motion - to lead to the termination
of commercial relations with Great Britain the following
year.[22]

Even though depression and political controversy
directly affected the working of the Meetings, other forces
might have been in operation in the 1770's. Was any alternative method developing to perform the functions of a central system of exchange for the decentralized agricultural
economy of Virginia? Were people finding it less necessary
to travel periodically to Williamsburg as Norfolk grew into
a business center for the lower Chesapeake area?

The important role of Norfolk in the grain trade
of the province has been demonstrated in an earlier chapter.

---

in the Eighteenth Century," Virginia Magazine of History and
Biography, XXXIX (1931), 233.

21. Arthur M. Schlesinger, The Colonial Merchants and
the American Revolution (New York: Columbia University
Press, 1918), pp. 135-138, 198-199, 236.

22. See ibid., pp. 362-370, 461-462, 509-519.

Even in the tobacco trade, this port was assuming significance in the 1770's.  By 1770, merchants were discussing
the relative advantages of loading tobacco at Norfolk or
on one of the major rivers.[23]  It was particularly advanta-
geous to load at Norfolk late in the season, when tobacco
might have to be collected from several points to assemble
a cargo.[24]

    With the growth of Norfolk's commerce came the
development of ancillary industries.  Shipyards provided
facilities for building all kinds of water craft, and ship-
builders contracted with British shippers as well as with
local merchants.[25]  Refitting provided work for ship

---

    23.  For example, Arthur Morson, manager of the Glass-
ford store at Falmouth, wrote to Jamieson in 1770: "If you
think proper to Load the Gordon [with tobacco] at Norfolk
I believe you need not send any more craft to Poto[mac].
...if you send her to this River w[i]t[h] a flat, I believe
she might be very expeditiously loaded...but you are the
best Judge whether pilotage & entry into this River would
ballance it or not."  Arthur Morson to Neil Jamieson, June
1, 1770, Papers of Neil Jamieson, XII, p. 2592.

    24.  A London merchant proposed to Jamieson in 1764
that his ship "should load at Norfolk & have Tob[acco]o
sent down from James, York & Rappa[hannock] & Potomack
River from any of your friends that have any Left."  Robert
& Robert Bogle & Scott to Neil Jamieson, June 3, 1764, ibid.,
IV, p. 752.

    25.  Mr. Munro to Neil Jamieson, May 13, 1761, ibid.,
I, p. 43.

carpenters, glaziers, iron-workers, coopers, and sail-
makers.[26] Other local industries included a distillery,
started in 1769 by local capitalists with an investment of
£5,400,[27] and a rope walk and tanyard. The latter owned
fourteen buildings and fifty slaves in 1774, and valued
its property at £16,800 sterling.[28]

    Whether further concentration of trade and shipping
at Norfolk would have resulted in that city's assuming
other functions of a metropolitan center of Virginia, particularly in financial business, is, of course, impossible
to determine, since Norfolk's most promising future was
shattered by the events of the American Revolution.

---

26. Thomas J. Wertenbaker, Norfolk: Historic Southern
Port (Durham: Duke University Press, 1931), p. 45.

27. Memorial of William Calderhead, American Loyalist
Transcripts (New York Public Library), LVIII, pp. 238-257.

28. Papers relating to business affairs and losses of
James Parker, Parker Family Papers (Liverpool Record Office),
bundle 16.

## CONCLUSION

To summarize briefly, the Williamsburg Meeting
of Merchants performed many of the functions of a metropolitan
center for the Virginia economy. The Meeting provided, most
importantly, a clearinghouse for financial transactions,
as well as something of a central market for the major export commodities of the colony. The structure of this
system of exchange differed considerably from that of the
modern metropolis, primarily because business in the Old
Dominion was so decentralized. Businessmen conducted their
day-to-day affairs, such as the purchase of tobacco and
wheat and the sale of merchandise, in the small communities
of the province. Even so, the political importance of Williamsburg gave that city a role in Virginia's economic life
that was of considerable significance prior to the American
Revolution.

APPENDIX A - EXPORTS FROM THE SEVEN DISTRICTS OF VIRGINIA, JANUARY 5, 1772 - JANUARY 5, 1773

| Product | | Great Britain | Ireland | Southern Europe & Wine Is. | Africa | W.Indies | Coastways | Total |
|---|---|---|---|---|---|---|---|---|
| Ashes - Pot | cwt. | 6 | | | | | | 6 |
| Pearl | tons | 6 | | | | | | 6 |
| Beer, Cyder, etc. | bbls. | | | | | 11 | 22 | 33 |
| Brass, old | lbs. | 350 | | | | | 200 | 550 |
| Bricks | no. | | | | | 8,700 | 111,500 | 120,200 |
| Candles - Spermacato | lbs. | | | 175 | | | | 175 |
| Tallow | lbs. | | | 200 | | 450 | 1,300 | 1,950 |
| Chocolate | lbs. | | | | 200 | | 5,406 | 5,606 |
| Cocoa | lbs. | | | | | | 2,400 | 2,400 |
| Coffee | cwt. | 18 | | | | | | 18 |
| Cotton | lbs. | 2,484 | | | | | 6,683 | 9,167 |
| Feathers | lbs. | | | | | | 5,192 | 5,192 |
| Flax | lbs. | | | | | | 1,772 | 1,772 |
| Flaxseed | bush. | 48 | 64 | | | | 2,297 | 2,409 |
| Furs - Fox | no. | | | | | | 1,800 | 1,800 |
| Mink | no. | | | | | | 25 | 25 |
| Otter | no. | | | | | | 100 | 100 |
| Furtick [Fustick?] | cwt. | 559 | | | | | | 559 |
| Gensing | lbs. | 4,670 | | | | | | 4,670 |
| Gin | cases | | | | | | 5 | 5 |
| | gals. | | | | | | 430 | 430 |
| Grain - Corn, Ind. | bush. | | | 72,071 | 4,699 | 304,431 | 180,367 | 561,568 |
| Oats | bush. | | | | | 7,896 | 5,419 | 13,315 |
| Rye | bush. | | | 300 | | | 2,047 | 2,347 |
| Wheat | bush. | 24 | 3,146 | 94,366 | | | 100,858 | 198,394 |
| Hemp | cwt. | | | | | | 52 | 52 |
| | cwt. | | | | | | 23 | 23 |
| Hides | cwt. | | | | | | 571 | 571 |

APPENDIX A (Cont'd)

| Product | | Great Britain | Ireland | Southern Europe & Wine Is. | Africa | W.Indies | Coastways | Total |
|---|---|---|---|---|---|---|---|---|
| Indigo | lbs. | 2,423 | | | | | | 2,423 |
| Iron - Bar | tons | 96 | | | | 17 | 45 | 158 |
| | cwt. | 27 | | | | 22 | 9 | 58 |
| Cast | cwt. | | | | | | 8 | 8 |
| | lbs. | | | | | | 82 | 82 |
| Pig | tons | 1,499 | 15 | | | | | 1,518 |
| | cwt. | 44 | | | | 4 | | 44 |
| Wrought-axes | no. | | | | | | 221 | 221 |
| | tons | | | | | 40 | | 40 |
| Lard | lbs. | | | | | 15,450 | 36,230 | 51,680 |
| Leather | lbs. | | | | | 251 | 5,000 | 5,251 |
| Lemons & oranges | no. | | | | | | 48 | 48 |
| Logwood | tons | 16 | | | | | | 16 |
| Lumber - boards & planks - Cedar | ft. | | | | | | 1,100 | 1,100 |
| Oak | ft. | 48,964 | | | | | | 48,964 |
| Pine | ft. | 30,359 | | 8,495 | | 2,027,368 | 7,790 | 2,074,012 |
| Handspikes | no. | 4,101 | 1,272 | | | 48 | | 5,421 |
| Hoops | no. | 9,388 | | | | 158,790 | | 168,178 |
| Lock Stocks | no. | 32,060 | | | | | | 32,060 |
| Oars | ft. | 21,265 | | | | 2,496 | | 23,761 |
| Shingles | no. | | | 75,380 | | 8,671,666 | 94,600 | 8,841,646 |
| Staves | no. | 2,681,220 | 78,000 | 53,260 | | 2,630,290 | 100,770 | 5,543,540 |
| Timber-Cedar | tons | 1 | | | | | 18 | 19 |
| | ft. | 32 | | | | | 62 | 94 |
| Oak | tons | 557 | | | | | | 557 |
| | ft. | 83 | | | | 68 | | 151 |
| Pine | tons | 183 | | | | | | 183 |
| | ft. | 12 | | | | | | 12 |
| Trunnells | no. | 4,100 | 3 | | | | | 4,103 |

APPENDIX A (Cont'd)

| Product | | Great Britain | Ireland | Southern Europe & Wine Is. | Africa | W. Indies | Coastways | Total |
|---|---|---|---|---|---|---|---|---|
| Mahogany | ft. | 3,680 | | | | | 642 | 4,322 |
| Meal | bush. | | | | | 546 | | 546 |
| Molasses | gals. | | | | | | 2,079 | 2,079 |
| Naval Stores - Pitch | bbls | 12 | | | | 134 | 51 | 197 |
| Tar | bbls | 21,138 | | | | 855 | 888 | 22,881 |
| Turpentine | bbls | 1,411 | | | | 2,894 | 808 | 5,113 |
| Masts | no. | 49 | | | | | | 49 |
| Oil, Train | gals. | | | | | | 94 | 94 |
| Ore, Copper | tons | 2 | | | | | | 2 |
| | cwt. | 16 | | | | | | 16 |
| Provisions - Beef & Pork | bbls. | | | | | 5,289 | 1,481 | 6,770 |
| Bread & Flour | tons | | 1 | 1,193 | 11 | 1,439 | 641 | 3,285 |
| | cwt. | 24 | 4 | 78 | 10 | 45 | 41 | 202 |
| Butter | lbs. | | | 910 | | 4,200 | 29,510 | 34,620 |
| Cheese | lbs. | | | | | | 200 | 200 |
| Fish - Dried | qls. | | | | | | 20 | 20 |
| Pickled | bbls. | | | 6 | | 3,183 | 836 | 4,025 |
| Hams | bbls. | | | | | 172 | | 172 |
| Peas, etc. | bush. | | | 1,679 | | 14,849 | 4,764 | 21,292 |
| Potatoes | bush. | | | | | | 1,327 | 1,327 |
| Rum - New England | gals. | 3,530 | | | | | 15,201 | 18,731 |
| West Indian | gals. | | | 540 | | | 40,472 | 41,012 |
| Salt | bush. | | | | | | 13,350 | 13,350 |
| Sassafras | cwt. | 99 | | | | | | 99 |
| Shoes | prs. | | | | | | 107 | 107 |
| Skins - Bear | no. | | | | | | 47 | 47 |
| Beaver | lbs. | 1,850 | | | | | | 1,850 |
| Deer - Dressed | no. | | | | | | 1,842 | 1,842 |
| | lbs. | 29,695 | | | | | | 29,695 |

APPENDIX A (Cont'd)

| Product | | Great Britain | Ireland | Southern Europe & Wine Is. | Africa | W.Indies | Coastways | Total |
|---|---|---|---|---|---|---|---|---|
| Skins (cont'd) | | | | | | | | |
| Deer - Raw | no. | | | | | | 6,029 | 6,029 |
| | lbs. | 144,657 | | | | | | 144,657 |
| Racoon | no. | 102 | | | | | | 102 |
| | lbs. | 900 | | | | | | 900 |
| Snakeroot | lbs. | | | | | | | |
| Soap | lbs. | | | | | 200 | 950 | 1,150 |
| Stock, Live-Horses | no. | | | | | 5 | | 5 |
| Sheep | no. | | | | | 20 | | 20 |
| Poultry | doz. | | | | | 57 | | 57 |
| Sugar - Loaf | lbs. | | | | | | 1,768 | 1,768 |
| Brown | cwt. | 680 | | | | | 329 | 1,009 |
| Tobacco | hhds. | 79,614 | | | | | | 79,614 |
| | lbs. | 84,755,274 | | | | 147,036 | 36,655 | 84,938,965 |
| Turtle | lbs. | | | | | | 200 | 200 |
| Walnut - Black -Boards | ft. | 9,650 | 3,939 | | | | 1,050 | 14,639 |
| Timber | tons | 46 | 1 | | | | | 47 |
| | ft. | 98 | | | | | | 98 |
| Wax - Bees | lbs. | | | 13,400 | | 2,600 | 11,430 | 27,430 |
| Myrtle | lbs. | | | | | | 1,600 | 1,600 |
| Whalefins | lbs. | 500 | | | | | | 500 |
| Wine | tons | 4 | | | | | | 4 |
| | gals. | 464 | | | | | 336 | 800 |

Source: North Manuscripts (Bodleian Library)

# BIBLIOGRAPHY

## MANUSCRIPT SOURCES

* Indicates that microfilm copy of manuscripts is located
  in Research Department, Colonial Williamsburg, Inc.

Allason, William
   Letters and papers, 1752-1779 (7 boxes)
   Letterbooks, 1757-1789 (2 volumes)
   [Virginia State Library Archives, Richmond, Virginia]

*American Loyalist Transcripts
   [New York Public Library, New York, New York]

*Anderson, Robert
   Letterbook, 1698-1715
   [University of Virginia, Charlottesville, Virginia]

*Atkinson, Roger
   Letterbook, 1769-1776
   [University of Virginia]

*Bassett Family Papers, 1693-1837
   [Library of Congress, Washington, D. C.]

Caroline County Appeals and Land Cases, 1787-1807
   [Virginia State Library Archives]

*Carter, Robert
   Letterbooks, 1772-1785 (6 vols.)
   [Duke University, Durham, North Carolina]

*Chalmers Collection, Volume IV
   [New York Public Library]

*Corbin, Richard
   Letterbook, 1758-1768
   [Colonial Williamsburg, Williamsburg, Virginia]

*Cunninghame, William, & Company
   Letterbooks, 1767-1773 (2 vols.)
   [National Library of Scotland, Edinburgh]

*Hook, John
   Papers, 1771-1784
   [Duke University]

*Jamieson, Neil
   Papers, 1757-1789 (23 vols.)
   [Library of Congress]

*Jerdone, Francis
   Ledger, 1751-1752
   [Colonial Williamsburg]

Jerdone, Francis
   Letterbooks, 1738-1744, 1756-1763, 1769-1776 (3 vols.)
   (Volume III is the Letterbook of Thomas Jett.)
   [College of William and Mary, Williamsburg, Virginia]

Miscellaneous letters and documents
   [Public Record Office, London]

*Nelson, Thomas and William
   Letterbook, 1766-1775
   [Virginia State Library]

North Papers
   Exports and imports from and to the ports of North
      America, January 5, 1772-January 5, 1773.
   [Bodleian Library, Oxford, England]

*Norton, John, & Sons
   Papers, 1752 (1768-1800) 1827
   [Colonial Williamsburg]

*Norton-Savage-Dickson
   Papers in Brock Collection
   [Huntington Library, San Marino, California]

*Palfrey, William
   Papers, 1763-1774
   [Harvard College Library, Cambridge, Massachusetts]

*Parker Family
   Papers, 1759-1835
   [Liverpool Record Office, Liverpool, England]

*Piper, Harry
   Letterbook, 1767-1775
   [University of Virginia]

Pleasants, Robert
   Letterbook, 1771-1778
   [College of William and Mary]

*Prentis, William
   Papers, 1733-1780
   [University of Virginia]

*Reynolds, William
   Letterbooks, 1771-1785 (2 vols.)
   [Library of Congress]

*Snelson, John
   Letterbook, 1757-1775
   [Southern Historical Collection, Chapel Hill,
      North Carolina]

*Steuart, Charles
   Letterbooks, 1751-1763 (2 vols.)
   [Historical Society of Pennsylvania, Philadelphia,
      Pennsylvania]

*Steuart, Charles
   Papers, 1758-1798 (21 vols.)
   [National Library of Scotland]

*Virginia Boxes, Miscellaneous
   Norfolk Committee of Correspondence to Baltimore
      Committee of Correspondence
   [New York Public Library]

*Wallace, Davidson, & Johnson
   Letterbooks, 1771-1777 (2 vols.)
   [Maryland Hall of Records, Annapolis, Maryland]

*Yates, Charles
   Letterbook, 1773-1783
   [University of Virginia]

PRINTED SOURCE MATERIALS

Anderson's Historical and Chronological Deduction of the
    Origin of Commerce,...Revised by Mr. Coombe.  6 vols.
    Dublin: P. Byrne, 1790.

"The Association in Williamsburg, in 1770," Virginia His-
    torical Register, III (1850), 17-24.

Carman, Harry J., ed. American Husbandry.  New York:
    Columbia University Press, 1939.

"A French Traveller in the Colonies, 1765," American His-
    torical Review, XXVI (1921), 726-747; XXVII (1922) 70-89.

Hening, William W., ed.  The Statutes at Large: being a
    Collection of All the Laws of Virginia.  13 vols.
    Richmond, 1810-1823.

"Jerman Baker to Duncan Rose," William and Mary Quarterly,
    1st ser., XII (1904), 237-242.

"John Banister to Elisha Tupper, July 11, 1775," Virginia
    Magazine of History and Biography, XXVIII (1920), 266-273.

"Journal of Alexander Macaulay," William and Mary Quarterly,
    1st ser., XI (1902), 180-191.

Koch, A. & Peden, W., eds.  The Life and Selected Writings
    of Thomas Jefferson.  New York:  Modern Library, 1944.

"Letter Book of Francis Jerdone," William and Mary Quarterly,
    1st ser., XI (1902), 153-160, 236-242.

"Letters of Robert Pleasants, of Curles," William and Mary
    Quarterly, 2d ser., I (1921), 107-113; II (1922), 257-275.

Mair, John.  Book-keeping Methodiz'd: or a Methodical Treatise
    of Merchant-Accompts.  2nd Ed.  Edinburgh: W. Sands, 1741.

Mason, Frances N., ed.  John Norton & Sons: Merchants of London
    and Virginia.  Richmond: Dietz Press, 1937.

"The Meeting of the Merchants, Held in Williamsburg, in 1770," Virginia Historical Register, III (1850), 79-83.

"Paper Money in Colonial Virginia," William and Mary Quarterly, 1st ser., XX (1912), 227-262.

[Tucker, St. George]. "A Letter to the Rev. Jerediah Morse," William and Mary Quarterly, 1st ser., II (1894) 181-203.

Wright, J. The American Negotiator, or the Various Currencies of the British Colonies in America. 3d ed. London: J. Smith, 1765.


NEWSPAPERS

Virginia Gazette (Parks), 1736-1750

Virginia Gazette (Hunter), 1751-1761

Virginia Gazette (Royle), 1761-1765

Virginia Gazette (Purdie & Dixon), 1766-1775

Virginia Gazette (Rind), 1766-1774

Virginia Gazette or, Norfolk Intelligencer, 1774-1775


SECONDARY WORKS

Albion, Robert G. The Rise of New York Port [1815-1860]. New York: Charles Scribner's Sons, 1939.

Ashton, T. S. An Economic History of England: The 18th Century. London: Methuen & Company, 1955.

Atherton, Lewis E. The Southern Country Store, 1800-1860. Baton Rouge: Louisiana State University Press, 1949.

Barbour, Violet. Capitalism in Amsterdam in the Seventeenth Century. Baltimore: Johns Hopkins Press, 1950.

Baxter, W. T.  The House of Hancock: Business in Boston
    1724-1775.  Cambridge: Harvard University Press, 1945.

Berg, Harry D.  "Merchants and Mercantile Life in Colonial
    Philadelphia, 1748-1763."  Unpublished Ph. D. disserta-
    tion, University of Iowa, 1941.

Berg, Harry D. "The Organization of Business in Colonial
    Philadelphia," Pennsylvania History, X (1943), 157-177.

Bezanson, Anne; Gray, Robert D; and Hussey, Miriam.  Prices
    in Colonial Pennsylvania.  Philadelphia: University of
    Pennsylvania Press, 1935.

Bridenbaugh, Carl.  Seat of Empire: The Political Role of
    Eighteenth-Century Williamsburg.  Williamsburg: Colonial
    Williamsburg, 1950.

Brock, Leslie Van Horn.  "Currency of the American Colonies,
    1700-1764: A Study in Colonial Finances and Imperial
    Relations."  Unpublished Ph. D. dissertation, University
    of Michigan, 1941.

Bruce, Philip A.  Economic History of Virginia in the Seven-
    teenth Century.  2 vols.  New York: Macmillan Company,
    1895.

Bruchey, Stuart.  "Success and Failure Factors: American
    Merchants in Foreign Trade in the Eighteenth and Early
    Nineteenth Centuries,"  Business History Review, XXXII
    (1958), 272-292.

Cabell, N. F.  "Some Fragments of an Intended Report on
    the Post Revolutionary History of Agriculture in Virginia,"
    with Notes by E. G. Swem, William and Mary Quarterly,
    1st ser., XXVI (1918), 145-168.

Chandler, Lester V.  Introduction to Monetary Theory.  New
    York: Harper & Brothers, 1940.

Channing, Edward.  A History of the United States.  6 vols.
    New York:  Macmillan Company, 1930-1938.

Chumbley, George L. Colonial Justice in Virginia: The Development of a Judicial System, Typical Laws and Cases of the Period. Richmond: Dietz Press, 1938.

Clapham, Sir John. The Bank of England: A History. 2 vols. Cambridge: Cambridge University Press, 1945.

Coakley, Robert W. "Virginia Commerce during the American Revolution." Unpublished Ph. D. dissertation, University of Virginia, 1949.

Cole, Arthur H. "Evolution of the Foreign-Exchange Market of the United States," Journal of Economic and Business History, I (1929), 386-421.

Coulter, Calvin B. "The Virginia Merchant." Unpublished Ph. D. dissertation, Princeton University, 1944.

Craven, Avery O. Soil Exhaustion as a Factor in the Argicultural History of Virginia and Maryland, 1606-1860. Urbana: University of Illinois, 1926.

Davis, Joseph S. Essays in the Earlier History of American Corporations. 2 vols. Cambridge: Harvard University Press, 1917.

Dickerson, Oliver M. The Navigation Acts and the American Revolution. Philadelphia: University of Pennsylvania Press, 1951.

East, Robert A. "The Business Entrepreneur in a Changing Colonial Economy, 1763-1795," Tasks of Economic History. Supplemental Issue of The Journal of Economic History, VI (1946), 16-27.

Evans, Emory G. "Planter Indebtedness and the Coming of the Revolution in Virginia," William and Mary Quarterly, 3d ser., XIX (1962), 511-533.

Feavearyear, A. E. The Pound Sterling: A History of English Money. Oxford: Clarendon Press, 1931.

Ferguson, E. James. "Currency Finance: An Interpretation of Colonial Monetary Practices," William and Mary Quarterly, 3d ser., X (1953), 153-180.

Flippin, Percy S.  The Royal Government in Virginia, 1624-1775.  New York: Columbia University Press, 1919.

Ford, Paul L., ed.  The Works of Thomas Jefferson.  12 vols.  New York: G. P. Putnam's Sons, 1904-1905.

Foulke, Roy A.  The Sinews of American Commerce.  New York: Dun & Bradstreet, Inc., 1941.

Fox Bourne, H. R.  English Merchants: Memoirs in Illustration of the Progress of British Commerce.  2 vols.  London: Richard Bentley, 1866.

Goodwin, Rutherfoord.  A Brief & True Report Concerning Williamsburg in Virginia.  Williamsburg: Colonial Williamsburg, 1940.

[Gourlay, James].  A Glasgow Miscellany: The Tobacco Period in Glasgow, 1707-1775.  n.p., n.d.

Gras, N. S. B.  Business and Capitalism: An Introduction to Business History.  New York: F. S. Crofts & Company, 1939.

Gras, N. S. B.  An Introduction to Economic History.  New York: Harper & Brothers, 1922.

Gray, Lewis C.  History of Agriculture in the Southern United States to 1860.  2 vols.  Washington: Carnegie Institution of Washington, 1933.

Gray, Lewis C.  "The Market Surplus Problems of Colonial Tobacco,"  Agricultural History, I (1928), 1-34.

Hamilton, H.  An Economic History of Scotland in the Eighteenth Century.  Oxford: Clarendon Press, 1963.

Hamilton, H.  "The Failure of the Ayr Bank, 1772,"  Economic History Review, 2d ser., VIII (1956), 405-417.

Hardy, Charles O.  "Market,"  Encyclopaedia of the Social Sciences.  15 vols.  New York: Macmillan Company, 1930-1934.

Harper, Lawrence A.  The English Navigation Laws.  New York: Columbia University Press, 1939.

Harper, Lawrence A. "The Effect of the Navigation Acts
    on the Thirteen Colonies," in The Era of the American
    Revolution, ed. Richard B. Morris. New York: Columbia
    University Press, 1939.

Harrell, Isaac F. Loyalism in Virginia. Durham: Duke
    University Press, 1926.

Harrington, Virginia D. The New York Merchant on the Eve
    of the Revolution. New York: Columbia University Press,
    1935.

Hedges, James B. The Browns of Providence Plantations:
    Colonial Years. Cambridge: Harvard University Press,
    1952.

Herndon, G. Melvin. "Hemp in Colonial Virginia," Agri-
    cultural History, XXXVII (1963), 86-93.

Jensen, Arthur L. The Maritime Commerce of Colonial
    Philadelphia. Madison: The State Historical Society
    of Wisconsin, 1963.

Joslin, D. M. "London Private Bankers, 1720-1785," Eco-
    nomic History Review, 2d ser., VI (1954), 167-186.

Lerner, A. P. "The Myth of the Parasitic Middleman,"
    Commentary, VIII (1949), 45-51.

Lipson, E. The Economic History of England. 3 vols.
    London: Adam & Charles Black, 1948.

Mays, David J. Edmund Pendleton, 1721-1803: A Biography.
    2 vols. Cambridge: Harvard University Press, 1952.

Middleton, Arthur P. Tobacco Coast: A Maritime History
    of Chesapeake Bay. Newport News: The Mariners' Museum,
    1953.

Minchinton, Walter E. "The Virginia Letters of Isaac
    Hobhouse, Merchant of Bristol," Virginia Magazine of
    History and Biography, LXVI (1958), 278-301.

Morton, Louis. Robert Carter of Nomini Hall. Williamsburg: Colonial Williamsburg, 1941.

Nettels, Curtis P. The Money Supply of the American
Colonies Before 1720. University of Wisconsin Studies
in the Social Sciences and History, Number 20. Madison,
1934.

Nussbaum, F. L. A History of the Economic Institutions
of Modern Europe. New York: F. S. Crofts & Company,
1935.

Pares, Richard. Merchants and Planters. Economic History
Review Supplement 4. Cambridge: Cambridge University
Press, 1960.

Pares, Richard. Yankees and Creoles: The Trade Between
North America and the West Indies before the American
Revolution. Cambridge: Harvard University Press, 1956.

Plummer, Wilbur C. "Consumer Credit in Colonial Philadelphia," Pennsylvania Magazine of History and Biography, LXVI (1942), 385-409.

Price, Jacob M. The Tobacco Adventure to Russia: Enterprise, Politics, and Diplomacy in the Quest of a
Northern Market for English Colonial Tobacco, 1676-
1722. Transactions of the American Philosophical
Society, new ser., vol. 51, pt. 1. Philadelphia, 1961.

Price, Jacob M. "The French Farmers-General in the Chesapeake: The MacKercher-Huber Mission of 1737-1738,"
William and Mary Quarterly, 3d ser., XIV (1957), 125-153.

Price, Jacob M. "The Rise of Glasgow in the Chesapeake
Tobacco Trade, 1707-1775," William and Mary Quarterly,
3d ser., XI (1954), 179-199.

Ripley, William Z. The Financial History of Virginia,
1609-1776. New York: Columbia College, 1893.

Rosenblatt, Samuel M. "The Significance of Credit in the
Tobacco Consignment Trade: A Study of John Norton &
Sons, 1768-1775," William and Mary Quarterly, 3d ser.,
XIX (1962), 383-399.

Schlesinger, Arthur M. The Colonial Merchants and the
American Revolution, 1763-1776. New York: Columbia
University Press, 1918.

Sellers, Leila. Charleston Business on the Eve of the
American Revolution. Chapel Hill: University of North
Carolina Press, 1934.

Sheridan, Richard B. "The British Credit Crisis of 1772
and the American Colonies," Journal of Economic History, XX (1960), 161-186.

Soltow, James H. "The Role of Williamsburg in the Virginia
Economy, 1750-1775," William and Mary Quarterly, 3d ser.,
XV (1958), 467-482.

Soltow, James H. "Scottish Traders in Virginia, 1750-1775,"
Economic History Review, 2d ser., XII (1959), 83-98.

Soltow, James H. "The Occupational Structure of Williamsburg in 1775." Typed manuscript report, Colonial
Williamsburg, Research Department, 1956.

Soltow, James H. "Thomas Riche's 'Adventure' in French
Guiana, 1764-1766." Pennsylvania Magazine of History
and Biography, LXXXIII (1959), 409-419.

Stephenson, Mary. "Brick House Tavern." Typed manuscript
report, Colonial Williamsburg, Research Department, 1956.

Stigler, George J. The Theory of Price. New York:
Macmillan Company, 1952.

Tatham, William. An Historical and Practical Essay on the
Culture and Commerce of Tobacco. London: Vernor & Hood,
1800.

Thayer, Theodore. "The Land-Bank System in the American
Colonies," Journal of Economic History, XIII (1953),
145-159.

Thomson, Edith E. B. "A Scottish Merchant in Falmouth in
the Eighteenth Century," Virginia Magazine of History
and Biography, XXXIX (1931), 108-117, 230-238.

Thomson, Robert P.  "The Merchant in Virginia, 1700-1775."
    Unpublished Ph. D. dissertation, University of Wis-
    consin, 1955.

Thomson, Robert P. "The Tobacco Export of the Upper James
    River Naval District, 1773-1775," William and Mary
    Quarterly, 3d ser., XVIII (1961), 393-407.

[Tyler, Lyon G.].  "Williamsburg - The Old Colonial Cap-
    ital," William and Mary Quarterly, 1st ser., XVI
    (1907), 1-65.

U. S. Bureau of the Census, Historical Statistics of the
    United States, Colonial Times to 1957.  Washington,
    D. C.: Government Printing Office, 1960.

Voke, A. F.  "Accounting Methods of Colonial Merchants
    in Virginia," Journal of Accountancy, XLII (1926),
    1-11.

Wertenbaker, Thomas J.  Norfolk: Historic Southern Port.
    Durham: Duke University Press, 1931.

Williamson, Arthur S.  "Credit Relations Between Colonial
    and English Merchants in the Eighteenth Century."  Un-
    published Ph. D. dissertation, University of Iowa, 1927.

Wyckoff, Vertrees J.  Tobacco Regulation in Colonial Mary-
    land.  Baltimore: Johns Hopkins Press, 1936.

Note:  This bibliography of secondary works is not
intended to be exhaustive of the literature bearing upon
the subject.  It lists the secondary works cited and
those found to be particularly useful.

INDEX

Coakley, Robert W., 2
Coastwise trade, 86-89, 187-190
Coins, foreign in Virginia, 109-111, Ta. XI, XII
Consignment, 33-41, 73-74
Corbin, Richard, 167
Corn, exported from Va., 76-79, 81, 86, 89;
    marketing of, 89-91, 94, 96, 97
Corn Laws, 78
Counterfeiting, 121-122
County courts, 13-14, 143-144
Courts, See County, Hustings
Craftsmen, 7
Credit system, 128-176
Culpeper Courthouse, 49, 51
Cuninghame, Alexander, 91
Cuninghame, William and Co., 51-54, 56, 57, 60, 61, 64,
    66, 73, 74, 75n, Ta. IX, X, 170
Cuninghame stores, 47, 48-49, Ta. VIII, 98, 99, 101,
    141, 152
Currency, shortage in Va., 107-112;
    values in colonies, Ta. XII


Davis, Mary, Mrs., 9
Debts, extent of in Virginia, 147-150
Depressions, 182-183
Dickson, Beverley, 154
Direct purchase, 41-45
Distilleries, 185
Douglas, Heron and Company, 154
Dumfries, 4, 49, 54, 67, 72, 73
Duncan, Stewart & Company, 87


Ellegood, Matthias, 59, 96
England, tobacco imports, 22n, Ta. IV
Exports, from England and Scotland, Ta. VII; from
    Virginia, 75-89, 187-190; from Virginia and
    Maryland, 21-22, Ta. I, II, III; tobacco from
    James River, 50
Europe, imports from Va., 81-86, 187-190

Tobacco, as money, 112-115; exported from England and
    Scotland, Ta. VII; knowledge of production
    necessary, 25-26; major export, 21-22, Ta. I, II,
    III; marketing of, 28-74; overproduction of, 22;
    prices, 44-48, 63-64, 65-74; purchased at county
    courts, 13-14; shipped from landing, 4; types of,
    22-24
Tobacco inspection, 26-28, 42, 113
Towns, 4-5
Trade, See Coastwise, Exports, Imports, Shipping
Trade, Committee of, 11
Tucker, St. George, 2
Turpentine, 76, 78, 86
Tyler, Lyon G., 2


Urbanna, 4


Vobe, Jane, 8


Warehouses, 4-5, 27
West Indies, imports from Va., 78-81, 187-190
Wheat, Corn Laws and, 78; exported from Virginia, 75, 78,
    81-82, 86-89; marketing of, 89-92, 94, 96; price of,
    97
Willing & Morris, 87-88, 170


York River, navigable distance, 3; tobacco exported
    from, Ta. III